HEROES OF THE SILVER SCREEN

Marlon Brando

HEROES OF THE SILVER SCREEN

Profiles of the sixteen top internationl stars – the Heroes of the Silver Screen – famous the world over for their acting and their screen appeal. How they started, how they made it: the fascinating facts, photographs in colour and black and white and up-to-date filmographies.

Edited by Michael Jay

Galahad Books · New York

Title page: Marlon Brando, studio portrait by John
Engstead, 1950

© 1982 Orbis Publishing Limited, London
Published by Galahad Books
95 Madison Avenue
New York, New York 10016

ISBN: 0-88365-629-9

Printed in Italy

Acknowledgments: Joel Finler Collection, Ronald
Grant Archive, Sally Hibbin, Kobal Collection,
National Film Archive, Talisman Books, Bob
Willoughby.

CONTENTS

6   Humphrey Bogart *by Oliver Eyquem*

10   Marlon Brando *by Richard Schickel*

14   Gary Cooper *by Margaret Hinxman*

18   Kirk Douglas *by Allan Eyles*

21   Clint Eastwood *by David Thomson*

25   Charlton Heston *by Jeffrey Richards*

28   Clark Gable *by DeWitt Bodeen*

32   Steve McQueen *by Phillip Bergson*

36   Paul Newman *by Michael Kerbel*

40   Laurence Olivier *by Sheridan Morley*

44   Gregory Peck *by Kingsley Canham*

48   Robert Redford *by Sally Hibbin*

52   Edward G. Robinson *by Colin McArthur*

55   James Stewart *by Richard Schickel*

58   Spencer Tracy *by Chester Erskine*

61   John Wayne *by Graham Fuller*

'Bogie'

Left: the quintessential Bogart 'look'. Top: the almost universally forgotten A Devil With Women (1930), co-starring Mona Maris, was Bogart's second feature film. Shortly after making it, he vowed never to return to Hollywood. Above: the vampiric title role in The Return of Dr X (1939) was Bogart's only flirtation with the horror film

The name perhaps means more things to more people than that of any other Hollywood hero. Bogart's ugly-handsome face, perpetual cigarette and rasping voice bespoke a man who was nobody's fool, a loner but never an outcast

Humphrey Bogart was born in New York on January 23, 1899. His father, Dr Belmont DeForest Bogart, was one of the city's most eminent surgeons. His mother, Maud Humphrey, was a magazine illustrator. After completing his studies at Trinity School, Bogart entered Phillips Acadamy in Andover, Massachusetts. Expelled for bad behaviour, he joined the US Marines in 1918 and served several months. On his return to civilian life, he was hired by the theatrical producer William A. Brady, who made him his road manager and encouraged him to try his hand at acting. His first appearances were somewhat unconvincing, but Bogart persevered and gradually learned to master the craft.

In 1929 he was spotted by a talent scout in *It's a Wise Child* and put under a year's contract by 20th Century-Fox. At this period he was just a young stage actor with no particular following; the studio, uncertain how best to use him, tried him out in an assortment of genres. The results were uneven and unpromising and Bogart, after being loaned out to Universal for a brief appearance in *Bad Sister* (1931) – as a man-about-town who leaves his young wife in the lurch – returned to Broadway, convinced that he was through with the cinema for good.

In December 1931, however, he signed a short-term contract with Columbia and left the stage to star in *Love Affair* (1932), a comedy directed by Thornton Freeland. He then moved to Warner Brothers where he made, for director Mervyn LeRoy, *Big City Blues* and *Three on a Match* (both 1932), the second of which provided him with his first gangster role. He then returned to the theatre.

The decisive turning-point in his hitherto erratic career came in 1935 with Robert E. Sherwood's play *The Petrified Forest*, in which, for more than seven months, he played the gangster Duke Mantee opposite Leslie Howard.

When asked to repeat his role on the screen the following year, Howard insisted on Bogart for his co-star. And so it was that, at the age of 37, Bogart finally gave up the theatre and began a profitable career as a supporting actor under the aegis of Warners, for which he would make almost all his films until 1948.

Plug ugly

He made an average of one film every two months for the studio, which filed him from the start under 'bad guys'. In four years he had completed an impressive number of gangster roles, supporting such established actors as Edward G. Robinson, James Cagney and George Raft. The parts he played – frequently double-crossers condemned to die an ignominious death – were most often used to set the main star off to advantage. These characters' backgrounds remained obscure and their psychology was extremely primitive. Several years had passed since *Little Caesar* (1930) and *The Public Enemy* (1931); the gangster was no longer seen as a romantic figure, he was just the flotsam of a sick society. Bogart, above all, played the kind of small-time loser who could always be outwitted by a strong adversary.

A few films, however, enabled him to escape from type-casting: *Isle of Fury* (1936), in which he was a reformed fugitive; *China Clipper* (1936), for which he donned the uniform of an ace pilot; and *Two Against the World* (1936), in which he played the manager of a radio station at odds with his unscrupulous employer. In *Marked Woman* (1937) he was a tough but kindly district attorney who succeeded in breaking up a gang of racketeers with the help of a nightclub hostess (Bette Davis); and in *Crime School* (1938), he was the liberal head of a prison, who established more humane relations between his staff and the troublesome young inmates.

These dissimilar roles, however, were not sufficient to modify the actor's predominant image, and it was not until Raoul Walsh's *They Drive by Night* (1940) that he was able to break out of the stereotype which had been imposed on him. Although his role was secondary to George Raft's, his playing of a truck-driver contending with the everyday problems of

Above left: as chief warden in Crime School *he had all kinds of problems with the Dead End Kids. Above right: in the gangster film* Brother Orchid *(1940) Bogart played his then usual role of a double-crosser. Right:* High Sierra *gave him the chance to show a human side. Below left: Bogart made a rare appearance in Western garb for* The Oklahoma Kid

travel fatigue and lack of money was concrete and recognizable. It reflected a realistic and documented context, and it embodied, however modestly, certain new attitudes to screen characterization.

In 1941, Bogart's luck suddenly changed for the better. He was given the lead in Walsh's *High Sierra* in place of George Raft (who had turned the part down). Although Ida Lupino had top billing (and gave one of her finest performances), it was Bogart, in the role of Roy Earle, an ageing and disillusioned gangster, who was the discovery of the film. For the first time he revealed a human dimension and depth which went beyond the requirements of the plot. Caught between loyalty to his old boss (who engineers his escape from prison for one last job) and the desire to start afresh with the young woman (Joan Leslie) whom he naively believes is in love with him, Roy is neither a hero nor a villain. He has a *history*, a past which weighs heavily on his present existence and offers him freedom only at the price of his own death.

The lone wolf

The Forties saw a radical change of direction in Bogart's career. As a result of the general anxiety caused by the war, the cinema gained in maturity, acquiring a new kind of gravity and urgency. *Film noir*, an eminently sceptical and ambiguous genre, came to the forefront and sought out heroes who would measure up to this increasingly troubled context. It was no longer an age for defying authority and not yet one for collective commitment. Neither gangster nor cop (but a little of both), the private eye asserted himself as one of the dominant heroic figures of the decade.

In 1941 this epitome of virile scepticism took on the features of Sam Spade. The character created in 1929 by the novelist Dashiell Hammett had already been twice adapted for the screen but without success; however the third version of *The Maltese Falcon*, which was more faithful than the others to Hammett's novel, hit the jackpot. Surrounded by a brilliant cast, Bogart perfectly illustrated the ethics of the private eye. Intransigent, totally independent, indifferent to the police yet wholly unself-serving, his Spade had absolute authenticity. The

Bogartian character had suddenly found its true physiognomy. He was, and would remain, a man who concealed his own needs behind a hard-bitten exterior, who rejected all higher principles and distrusted all abstract causes. He was a loner, who did not ask help from anyone.

Casablanca (1942) and *To Have and Have Not* (1944) both cast him in the midst of a cosmopolitan and divided world. In these films, fascists, Gaullists and refugees of every kind attempt to obtain his support but Bogart remains very much his own man. He acts solely according to his own inclinations: out of loyalty to a woman he has not forgotten (Ingrid Bergman in *Casablanca*) or to keep the love of the girl who has succeeded in winning his heart (Lauren Bacall in *To Have and Have Not*).

Cherchez la femme

Walsh had endowed Bogart with humanity in *High Sierra*; Huston gave him morality and the means to defend himself in *The Maltese Falcon*; Curtiz, in *Casablanca*, added to these a romantic dimension and a reason for living. At the beginning of the film, Rick, the hero, is shown to have taken refuge behind a mask of cynicism, in keeping with the unscrupulous political climate of wartime Casablanca. The unexpected arrival of the woman he has loved painfully reawakens his emotions, forcing him to renounce his pose of disinterested spectator. The film concludes with the need for commitment, one which concerned not only the hero but the whole of America. This moral framework reappears in *To Have and Have Not* in

Carrolls. These off-beat performances had only a limited impact in comparison with *The Big Sleep* (1946), in which Bogart, once more working with Hawks and Bacall, played another mythical detective: Philip Marlowe.

Trouble is his business

Created by Raymond Chandler in the late Thirties, Marlowe was a more romantic character than Spade. More directly implicated in the action, more conscious of the values which he represented, he was engaged in a quest for 'hidden truth'. Without being a paragon of virtue he had a rigorous conception of honour. No other actor would catch as precisely as Bogart this character's blend of strength and derision, or his equivocal pleasure in venturing down the 'mean streets' and daily facing death.

As Bogart himself became a mythical figure, he would meet up with replicas of his former self. In *Key Largo* (1948) Bogart played, opposite Lauren Bacall, a role analogous to Leslie Howard's in *The Petrified Forest*, while Edward G. Robinson played a mean gangster reminiscent of Duke Mantee. There was the same kind of allusive interplay in *The Treasure of the Sierra Madre* (1948), in which John Huston offered Bogart one of the most unusual roles of his career: as an adventurer on the skids, who sets off in search of gold and meets a squalid death, a victim of his own greed. The casting of Bogart against type disconcerted audiences when the film was released but, little by little, the actor managed to make himself accepted in character roles.

The last seven years of his career saw him gradually abandon heroic parts. With the exception of *Beat the Devil* (1953), in which Huston attempted a parodic approach to Bogart's screen persona, the majority of his films were well-received, proving that the actor had established a lasting and authentic relationship with his fans.

As the producer at the head of his own company, Santana Pictures, Bogart made *Knock on Any Door* (1949), a socially conscious film which took a firm stand against capital punishment. Then, after two conventional action films, *Tokyo Joe* (1949) and *Chain Lightning* (1950), he played the part of a disenchanted

which the hero, Harry Morgan, is caught between the temptation of detachment and the need to struggle against fascism. But the motives for which Harry finally resolves upon action remain strictly personal. The director Howard Hawks, as was his custom, reduced plot and action to the minimum and emphasized the romantic banter of Bogart and Lauren Bacall. As their on-screen romance became genuine love, Hawks reworked entire sequences day after day to explore their remarkable chemistry. The narrative thus gives a marvellous impression of authenticity and intimacy, and the film remains one of the highlights of Bogart's career.

In 1945 Bogart, whose previous wives had been actresses Helen Menken, Mary Phillips and Mayo Methot, married Lauren Bacall, who was then 21 and would be his greatest partner. Since 1943 and the box-office triumph of *Casablanca*, Bogart had become one of the top ten Hollywood stars. The end of the war saw him return to *film noir*. In 1945 he twice played the role of a murderer: opposite Alexis Smith in *Conflict* and Barbara Stanwyck in *The Two Mrs*

Hollywood screenwriter who is subject to attacks of murderous violence in Nicholas Ray's *In a Lonely Place* (1950). In *The Enforcer* (1951) he was a district attorney up against Murder Inc. Shot in the semi-documentary style typical of Warners, it became a *film noir* classic, particularly remarkable for the complexity of its editing and its powerful scenes of violence. (Twenty years later it was discovered that the film's direction, credited to Bretaigne Windust, was the work of Raoul Walsh.)

After the fourth, last and most disappointing film for Santana, *Sirocco* (1951), Bogart worked with Huston on *The African Queen* (1951). Half comedy of character, half adventure movie, totally and unashamedly implausible, the whole film was constructed on the confrontation of two personalities. Bogart gave one of his most colourful performances as a grouchy alcoholic transformed into a hero by a frigid, devout spinster (Katharine Hepburn) in the throes of her first amorous stirrings. That year, the actor received an Oscar, a reward honouring 20 years of a richly successful career. Modestly Bogart declared: 'I've been around a

long time. Maybe the people like me.'

With *Deadline USA* (1952), a vibrant plea for the freedom of the press, Bogart, with the director Richard Brooks, returned to the democratic inspiration of *Key Largo* and *Knock on Any Door*. The following year, Brooks cast him in *Battle Circus* as a sceptical and gruff military doctor, overfond of women and alcohol. In *The Caine Mutiny* (1954), an ambitious Stanley Kramer production directed by Edward Dmytryk, Bogart took on the part of Captain Queeg, a neurotic, dictatorial officer forcibly removed from command by his subordinates. The film was an ambiguous reflection on power and responsibility, in which the actor created an unusual character role. In Billy Wilder's *Sabrina* (1954) he was the sarcastic heir of a rich family in love with his chauffeur's daughter (Audrey Hepburn). Made in the same year, Joseph L. Mankiewicz's *The Barefoot Contessa*, one of the most fascinating evocations of the world of Hollywood, definitively made Bogart an outsider, a witness. He plays a film director, Harry Dawes, who watches the dazzling rise to stardom of a Spanish dancer (Ava Gardner)

and her tragic involvement with an impotent aristocrat. The narrator and spectator of action in which he cannot intervene, Dawes is the voice of Mankiewicz himself, the director's disillusioned double who embodies the magic of a vanished Hollywood. The actor's creased, serene face and understated performance brought both an exceptional resonance and a poignant sense of authenticity to the subject.

The commercial failure of the film, which was considered too literary at the time, led Bogart to return to more conventional roles in films of less interest: in Curtiz's *We're No Angels* (1955) he was a comic convict in company with Aldo Ray and Peter Ustinov; in Dmytryk's *The Left Hand of God* (1955) a sham priest taking refuge in a Chinese mission-house to escape the tyrannical war-lord whose adviser he has been. In William Wyler's *The Desperate Hours* (1955), already ravaged by the illness of which he was to die, Bogart played his last gangster role.

The long goodbye

In 1956 Mark Robson's *The Harder They Fall* cast him once more as a journalist, this time denouncing the boxing racket. Similar in mood to *Deadline USA*, it ended his career, if not in glory, then on an appropriately high note.

Bogart's relatively slow start was rapidly compensated for by the depth and variety of his roles from 1941 onwards. If the war years stand out by virtue of *The Maltese Falcon*, *Casablanca* and *To Have and Have Not*, after the war he was much freer in his choice of roles and was equally brilliant in socio-political films, thrillers and comedies. His last films reveal an actor totally identifying with his roles, enriching them with his own maturity, his unique capacity for understatement and irony.

Humphrey Bogart died of cancer on January 14, 1957. During the Sixties his reputation never ceased to grow until it reached the proportions of a cult. He possessed elegance, courage and insolence, and knew how to efface himself when necessary. Aggressive, precise, economical, his acting was astonishingly modern. Bogart remains today linked with the best that the American cinema has had to offer.
OLIVIER EYQUEM

Filmography
1930 Broadway's Like That/Ruth Etting in Broadway's Like That (short); Up the River; A Devil With Women. **'31** Body and Soul; Bad Sister; A Holy Terror. **'32** Love Affair; Big City Blues; Three on a Match. **'34** Midnight. **'36** The Petrified Forest; Bullets or Ballots; Two Against the World (USA retitling for TV: One Fatal Hour) (GB: The Case of Mrs Pembrook); China Clipper; Isle of Fury; The Great O'Malley. **'37** Black Legion; Marked Woman; Kid Galahad (USA retitling for TV: The Battling Bellhop); San Quentin; Dead End; Stand-In. **'38** Swing Your Lady; Men Are Such Fools; Crime School; Racket Busters; The Amazing Dr Clitterhouse; Angels With Dirty Faces. **'39** King of the Underworld; The Oklahoma Kid; You Can't Get Away With Murder; Dark Victory; The Roaring Twenties; The Return of Dr X; Invisible Stripes. **'40** Virginia City; It All Came True; Brother Orchid; They Drive by Night (GB: The Road to Frisco). **'41** High Sierra; The Wagons Roll at Night; The Maltese Falcon. **'42** All Through the Night; The Big Shot; Across the Pacific; Casablanca. **'43** Action in the North Atlantic; Thank Your Lucky Stars (guest); Sahara. **'44** Passage to Marseille; To Have and Have Not. **'45** Conflict; The Two Mrs Carrolls; Hollywood Victory Canteen (guest) (short). **'46** The Guys From Milwaukee (uncredited guest) (GB: Royal Flush); The Big Sleep. **'47** Dead Reckoning; Dark Passage; Always Together (uncredited guest). **'48** The Treasure of the Sierra Madre; Key Largo. **'49** Knock on Any Door; Tokyo Joe. **'50** Chain Lightning; In a Lonely Place. **'51** The Enforcer (GB: Murder Inc.); Sirocco; The African Queen. **'52** Deadline USA (GB: Deadline). **'53** Battle Circus; Beat the Devil (GB-IT). **'54** The Love Lottery (uncredited guest) (GB); The Caine Mutiny; A Star Is Born (voice only); Sabrina (GB: Sabrina Fair); The Barefoot Contessa. **'55** We're No Angels; The Left Hand of God; The Desperate Hours. **'56** The Harder They Fall.

Top left: an experienced prospector (Walter Huston) frowns grimly as his partner (Bogart) exhibits all the symptoms of gold fever in The Treasure of the Sierra Madre. *Below left: a 25-year gap in their ages did not prevent the marriage of Humphrey Bogart and Betty (Lauren) Bacall from being one of the happiest between two stars. Below: the cast of* The Caine Mutiny *(including Bogart, left, and Van Johnson, right) joke between takes*

A Rebel Named Brando

When Marlon Brando went to Hollywood his challenging style of acting became the controversial symbol of new hopes for American culture. Since the Fifties, he has brought to the screen a range of memorable characters – from Stanley Kowalski to Superman's father

Nowadays, one approaches a performance by Marlon Brando with a certain trepidation. Will he have bothered to learn his lines, or will he, as is his recent want, pin bits and pieces of the script to the set, so that the problem of memorization will not, as he claims, interfere with the process of creation? Will he be merely overweight, or will he be completely grossed out – as he was in *Apocalypse Now* (1979)? Will he focus his full concentration on the role, or will he content himself with what amounts to self-parody?

It seemed for a short time in the early Seventies, after *The Godfather* (1972) and *Ultimo Tango a Parigi* (1972, *Last Tango in Paris*), that he had not merely returned to form, but attained a new one – an ability to literally act his age – and that such tense questions might finally be rendered moot. Ah, foolish optimism! How could we have forgotten that the very basis of his screen character, the source of its fascination, lies in his childishly erratic, entirely anarchical nature. Brando would not be Brando if you could count on him. From the beginning we have attended his work not in search of seamless technical perfection, but as we do a thrill act at a carnival. We go to see him dive down into the depths of himself, to see if he will surface with some new pearls of existential awareness or a heap of rusting mannerism or, more likely, a

couple of the former mixed with a lot of the latter. If you cannot stand the sometimes instantaneous alternations between exasperation and exhilaration which he thus induces, then you have no business at a Brando film – which is, of course, a position many have adopted.

About the deepest sources of his wild ways one can only speculate. But about one of the matters that has driven him crazy, right from the start of his career, there can be no doubt. That is his unsought position as a hero of a special modern sort, a *cultural* hero, burdened with the large, if ill-defined, hopes of at least two generations for the renewal of American acting, and through it, of the American theatre, American films, perhaps even of American culture. It was not a role he sought! It was, indeed, a role he fought. And yet, somehow, it settled upon him.

Brando's Method

Brando, a high-school dropout, came more or less accidentally to acting, and he enjoyed an early success in it before developing a sense of vocation. He was thus forced to confront the personal and public demands of his profession without an aesthetic or a sense of cultural tradition. This gap was filled by the 'Method', that American variation on Stanislavky's theories, which was very much in the air in

New York when Brando was breaking into the theatre. Emerging from small parts into the unforgettable glory of his Stanley in *A Streetcar Named Desire*, he was seen as the personification of 'Method' principles (though, in truth, he had passed only briefly through its cathedral, the Actors' Studio). And since his own instinctive method – a search through memory for psychological truth, a rejection of classic manner and technique, squared with the 'Method', ('You have to upset yourself! Unless you do you cannot act'), the role of leader in a generational revolt was imposed upon him. American provincialism was to be shaken off; English acting standards would no longer go unchallenged.

Many in the older generation were appalled, but if you were young and cared about the mystery of acting, then Brando's singularity – there really never had been anyone quite like him – exercised a powerful symbolic hold on your imgination. Indeed, some part of you became his forever. And when he went out to Hollywood, hope mingled with fear over what would result. Would he revolutionize the place, or succumb to it. In the event, he remained . . . himself. That is to say, volatile and difficult, brilliant and indifferent. But there was no gainsaying the impact of his work in those first films, which were widely variable in their overall quality: the crippled war veteran in *The Men* (1950), the brutal Stanley Kowalski in *A Streetcar Named Desire* (1951), the Mexican revolutionary in *Viva Zapata!* (1952), the motorbike rebel in *The Wild One* (1953) and the ex-boxer in *On the Waterfront* (1954) – in these pictures he gave us moments which had never been seen on the screen before. For young

Opposite page: one of the exciting aspects of Marlon Brando's acting is his ability to transform his whole presence into the character he is portraying – from Stanley Kowalski in A Streetcar Named Desire *(far left) to the Mafia chief in* The Godfather *(left). Right: for* The Men, *he spent some weeks in a wheelchair learning how it feels to be a paraplegic. It was his first chance to try Method acting on the screen*

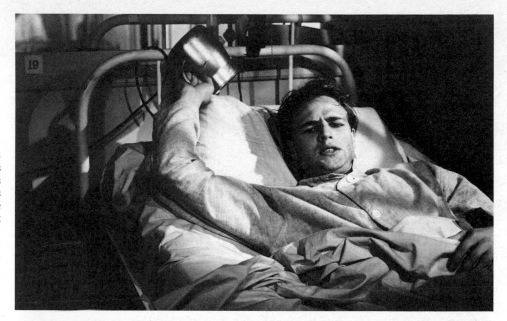

people his sullen, inarticulate rebelliousness won them to him forever. Even when he was playing brutes and dummies you sensed his vulnerability, his tentativeness, and, even, his underlying sweetness and sense of comedy. He was the first movie star who showed, right there on the screen, the truth behind the image – the insecurity and the nagging, peculiarly American fear that acting may not be suitable work for a grown-up heterosexual male. He was exploring what no-one else had explored.

In his first great role, that of Stanley Kowalski in *A Streetcar Named Desire*, people identified Brando with the image he played. Few heard him when he said:

'Kowalski was always right, and never afraid . . . He never wondered, he never doubted. His ego was very secure. And he had that kind of brutal aggressiveness I hate . . . I'm afraid of it. I detest the character.'

Stanley was crass, calculating and materialist – a type who was a factor in every aspect of American life in this century. The power of Brando's performance derives from his hatred and fear of the character, though manifestly there is something of Brando's own egotism and rudeness in Stanley too.

Winds of change

Brando found Hollywood – a town always full of Kowalskis – in a state of transition. The reliable mass market was slipping away to television; the factory system, ruled by a handful of industry 'pioneers', was losing its sovereignty to stars and directors who were, with the help of powerful agencies, creating their own packages. Brando had a long-term contract with Fox, but he fought the studio constantly and, unlike the older generation of stars, had the option to make independent films, so he could not be disciplined by suspensions or blacklisting. In addition he did not dress like a star, could not be coerced into interviews or publicity gimmicks he found demeaning. 'The only thing an actor owes his public is not to bore them' he declared.

The men who ruled Hollywood, quite rightly, distrusted Brando. They might talk about his manner and style (or lack of it) but deep down, they knew he was on to them, was parodying them on the screen. Still, through *On the Waterfront* an uneasy truce was maintained between Brando and Hollywood, if only because until that picture was finished – and they rewarded him with an Oscar – he stuck close to the type they had decided was correct for him and which was easily saleable – brooding, capable of brutality, yet gropingly sensitive and rebellious. Indeed, Terry Malloy, the ex-boxer, betrayed by his brother in *On the Waterfront*, seemed to many at the time a painfully accurate projection of Brando's own mood. When he says 'I could have been a contender . . . instead of a bum', some took this as an admission that the great roles were not for him. Others saw it as a generational

Above: Brando brought new depth – and an English accent – to Fletcher Christian, the officer who confronts Captain Bligh (Trevor Howard) in Mutiny on the Bounty. *Left: One Eyed Jacks shows up the images of male strength and violence used in Westerns*

lament, a declaration of betrayal not merely by an institution, but by the whole society in which humane, liberal values now seemed inadequate to a monstrously complex age.

Nevertheless, he won an Academy Award for *On the Waterfront* and continued to maintain himself as his contemporaries hoped he would – an inner-directed man in an other-directed world. There was, however, one big change in him. He no longer wanted to play roles that were projections of himself or even of his earlier image. In Terry Malloy he had achieved a kind of apotheosis; he now wanted to prove he could submerge self in characters. He undertook a staggering variety of roles from 1954 onwards: a Damon Runyon gambler in *Guys and Dolls* (1955); Napoleon in *Desiree* (1954); Sakini, the Japanese interpreter in *The Teahouse of the August Moon* (1956), the Southern soldier fighting his own racial prejudice in *Sayonara* (1957); the German soldier undergoing self-induced de-Nazification in *The Young Lions* (1958); the vengeful good-bad man in *One Eyed Jacks* (1961) and Fletcher Christian in *Mutiny on the Bounty* (1962).

Some of these pictures were successful at the box-office; some were not. There was a steady muttering about his waste of himself in subjects that, for the most part, were drawn from the less exalted ranges of popular fiction. In fact, he was playing a higher risk game than the critics knew, for his price was now something like a million dollars a picture in return for which he was supposed, by his presence, to guarantee a profit. What other actor would have risked that status in roles which were deliberately off-type and which caused him to use weird makeups and strange accents?

Gillo Pontecorvo, who directed him in *Queimada!* (1969, *Burn!*), declared, 'I never saw an actor before who was so afraid of the camera.' His hatred of publicity, his desire to hide-out in roles was based, in part, on simple shyness. Moreover, the kind of acting he was now doing demanded less of him emotionally, if more of him technically. As he said:

'There comes a time in one's life when you don't want to do it anymore. You know a scene is coming where you'll have to cry and scream and all those things, and it's always bothering you, always eating away at you . . . and you just can't walk through it . . . it would be disrespectful not to try to do your best.'

So he settled for imitations of life, which was not only easy for him, but fun. Acting at this level, he has been heard to say, is 'a perfectly reasonable way to make your living. You're not stealing money, and you're entertaining people'.

Other pressures came from the financial expectations of the industry. Directing *One Eyed Jacks*, he went way over budget, perhaps because he thought directing was a way of making an artistic statement without exposing so much of himself. The result was a lovely and violent film but still, to most people, just another Western.

Mutiny on 'Mutiny'

He might have escaped that set-back unscathed had he not followed it with *Mutiny on the Bounty*. There was a certain logic in the casting – Brando, the famous rebel, playing Fletcher Christian, the famous rebel. The trouble was that Brando insisted on playing Christian, not as a he-man of principle, as Clark Gable had, but as a foppish idler, with homosexual overtones, a character whose previously dormant sense of class difference, the basis of order in the British navy, turns torpid under Tahiti's tropical skies. It was not at all what the producers had in mind for a multi-million-dollar film on which MGM was depending for survival.

They claimed it was Brando's temperament that cost them an extra $10 million, but he was, in fact, taking the rap for all kinds of mismanagement, which included sending cast and crew off to shoot in the rainy season without a finished script in hand. Of course, Brando was angry and of course he turned as mutinous as Christian himself had.

What got lost in the resulting controversy was the fact that Brando's Christian was one of his finest sustained performances, a daring attempt to blend the humorous with the heroic, a projection of a modern, ironic sensibility backward into history. There was no-

thing cool or held back in this characterization; Brando took it right up to the hot edge of farce. If he was out of key with the rest of the players and the square-rigged plot, he actually did what a star is supposed to do, hold our interest in a big dumb remake – while risking comparison with the remembered performance of a beloved actor in a beloved role.

After *Mutiny on the Bounty*, came the deluge – poor parts, not a few of which he walked out on. In some of these films one can see the germ of the idea that attracted Brando: the chance to confront comedy directly in *Bedtime Story* (1964) and *A Countess From Hong Kong* (1967); the opportunity to make social comments he considered worthy in *The Ugly American* (1963), *The Chase* (1966) and *Queimada!*; even roles that matched his gift, despite their flawed context, notably that of the repressed homosexual army officer in *Reflections in a Golden Eye* (1967).

There are in these films isolated moments where Brando shines through. There is the scene in *Sayonara*, for example, when he confesses to his commanding general (and would-be father-in-law) that he is throwing

Top: in The Chase, *Bubber Reeves (Robert Redford) is arrested by the sheriff (Brando) but is shot – like Lee Harvey Oswald – before he can be tried. Directed by Arthur Penn,* The Chase *is a highly political film of bigotry and violence in the Deep South. Above: Brando plays a disillusioned English adventurer in* Queimada! *– a film about slavery and the colonization of the Caribbean*

over his fiancée for a Japanese girl. He conveys his anguish over this decision by picking up a cushion and concentrating on it the entire time they talk – a perfectly observed banal gesture. In *Reflections in a Golden Eye*, there is the scene when he thinks Robert Forster is coming to pay a homosexual call on him and he absurdly pats down his hair and smiles vainly to himself. Then there is *The Nightcomers* (1971) in which he hides out behind an Irish brogue and spends a lot of time indulging a bondage fetish with the governess, when, in the midst of it, he tells the children a long tall story and suddenly he's alive and playful and inventive, giving himself pleasure and making us share in it.

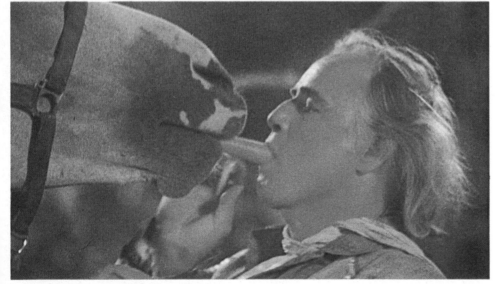

Left: light relief from Brando and Maria Schneider as the couple who share a frenentic sexual relationship in Last Tango In Paris. *Below left: in* The Missouri Breaks *(1976), Brando is a lawman – a typical John Wayne character – who, in this scene, shares a carrot with his horse before declaring his undying love for her. Above: the deranged Major Kurtz from* Apocalypse Now

nities. There is also in him something of the youthful, public Brando – self-romanticizing, self-pitying, yet self-satirizing too. All Brando's character Paul does in the film is have a restorative affair with a much younger woman. In the last sequences he is restored to a handsomeness that can be termed nothing less than beauty, a vitality, even a romantic energy, that is both miraculous and moving.

In the brilliant monologue at his dead wife's bier, perhaps the single greatest aria of his career, it all comes together, talent and technique, to express the violent ambivalence of his relationship with not merely this woman, but with himself and the world at large.

It was Brando's art, not director Bertolucci's, that made the highly melodramatic ending – in which, for no good reason, the star must die – a triumph. Brando removes the sting of death by the simple act of removing his chewing gum from his mouth and placing it neatly under the railing of the terrace where he takes his final fall – the tiny, perfect bit of actor's business, neatly undercutting the director's strain for a big finish.

Perhaps only a young director, cognizant of what Brando has meant to his generation, a director who self-consiously stripped from his work all intellectual and artistic traditions other than that of the cinema, could give his age's great *movie* actor this unprecedented opportunity for self-portraiture.

RICHARD SCHICKEL

But it was *The Godfather* that provided the long-awaited proof that he could still do most of it as an actor. He went after the part; even submitted to the indignity of a test. The result was a sustained characterization that depended for its success on more than a raspy voice and a clever old man's makeup. There were in his very movements, the hints of mortality that men in their forties begin to feel no matter how youthfully they maintain their spirits. His manner epitomized all the old men of power who had leaned across their desks to bend the young actor to their will – their wile and strength sheathed in reasonableness, commands presented in the guise of offers it *is*

hard to refuse. It was the culmination of his second career as a character man.

What one really wondered, though, was whether he had it in him to go all the way down the well again, come out from behind the masks and show again the primitiveness and power of his youth. That, quite simply, is what he did in *Last Tango in Paris*. Brando was playing physically what he is psychologically, an expatriate from his native land. Moreover, he was playing a man passing through the 'male menopause'. Yet in his sexual brutality there is something of Stanley Kowalski, and, like Terry Malloy, he is a one-time boxer, vulnerable in his mourning for lost opportu-

Filmography
1950 The Men. '**51** A Streetcar Named Desire. '**52** Viva Zapata! '**53** Julius Caesar; The Wild One. '**54** On the Waterfront; Desiree. '**55** Guys and Dolls. '**56** The Teahouse of the August Moon. '**57** Sayonara. '**58** The Young Lions. '**60** The Fugitive Kind. '**61** One Eyed Jacks (+prod; +dir). '**62** Mutiny on the Bounty. '**63** The Ugly American. '**64** Bedtime Story. '**65** Morituri (GB: The Saboteur – Code Name 'Morituri'). '**66** The Chase; The Appaloosa (GB: Southwest to Sonora). '**67** A Countess From Hong Kong (GB); Reflections in a Golden Eye. '**68** Candy (USA-FR-IT); The Night of the Following Day. '**69** Queimada! (USA: Burn!) (IT-FR). '**71** The Nightcomers (GB). '**72** The Godfather; Ultimo Tango a Parigi (USA/GB: Last Tango in Paris) (IT-FR). '**76** The Missouri Breaks. '**78** Superman, the Movie (GB). '**79** Apocalypse Now. '**80** The Formula.

Gary Cooper

The
Gentle
Giant

'Wyatt Earp, now, he hardly ever shot a man. But he frequently used to hit them between the eyes with the butt of his pistol. Don't know how he got away with it.'

He learned to sit tall in the saddle because of a road accident which damaged his hip. The doctor advised him that the best therapy would be horse-riding, a pastime at which he became skilled.

During his time at college – where he also developed his skill as a cartoonist – he thought he'd like to join the staff of a newspaper. By then his parents were living in Los Angeles, and Cooper was strolling down Hollywood Boulevard when he met a couple of chums who were playing extra roles in cheap Westerns for $10 a day. He decided to join them.

From 1925 Cooper appeared briefly in countless films. Then in 1927, Clara Bow – who had been having a much-publicized romance with Cooper – managed to secure him a minor role in Wings, directed by William Wellman, where he played an easy-going but doomed young flyer in World War I. The idea of heroically dying for one's country and the philosophy that what will be will be, were easy for Cooper to convey. In barely more than five minutes screen time he communicated a magnetism

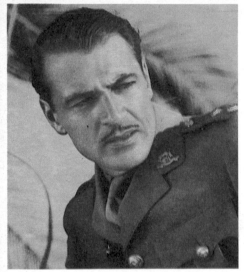

Previous page: Cooper in The Westerner *(1940). Top:* Wings *gave him the vital break at Paramount. Above: he played a similarly dashing young hero in* The Lives of a Bengal Lancer. *Below:* The Plainsman *(1936) put Cooper's horsemanship to good use.*

More than any other actor, Gary Cooper epitomized the quiet, staunch, gallant virtues of the pioneer American as portrayed in the cinema. The Western hero of *The Virginian* (1929) and *High Noon* (1952) was, in principle, not so different from the rebellious adventurer of *The Lives of a Bengal Lancer* (1935) or the hick-from-the-sticks who becomes a crusading millionaire in *Mr Deeds Goes to Town* (1936).

Within a certain range, from comedy to near-documentary drama, he was a peerless film performer. Ernest Hemingway insisted he play the lead in *For Whom the Bell Tolls* (1943) because he was the perfect Hemingway hero, a man who could fight the good fight and still retain his own integrity and dignity.

John Barrymore observed: 'That fellow is the world's greatest actor. He can do with no effort what the rest of us spent years trying to learn – to be perfectly natural.'

Certainly he was one of the first actors who achieved an instant rapport with the camera.

At the height of his popularity in the Thirties and Forties, he tended to be regarded as a 'personality' actor, who always played the same role in different settings. Later, his performances were reassessed. Because he appeared so 'natural', the public and even the critics believed he was simply playing himself. But, as countless stars have said, playing yourself is the most difficult art in the cinema.

He was born in 1901, the son of British immigrants. His father was a judge who owned a ranch. Gary was christened Frank, the name Gary being bestowed on him later by an agent. They lived in Helena, Montana, which Cooper remembered when it was a goldmining town – called Last Chance Gulch. During the making of his penultimate film, *The Wreck of the Mary Deare* (1959), he reminisced about the old days:

'I saw a gunfight once; a couple of characters had had a fight, gone home and thought about it, then they met up in town and shot it out. My pal and I were standing on the street outside the saloon. Darn near got shot, too.'

He never liked the idea of Westerns which were based on the legend of the fastest draw:

Above: Cooper with Helen Hayes in A Farewell to Arms, *after which he became a close friend of author Ernest Hemingway.*

who was only concerned about how his protégée, Dietrich, would look.

Hollywood didn't really know what to do with Cooper in the Thirties. Incredibly handsome, he also conveyed a toughness that was evident in his eyes. Helen Hayes – who co-starred with him in the first film version of Hemingway's *A Farewell to Arms* (1932) – remembers him as 'the most beautiful man I have ever met'.

In 1936 he established a professional relationship with director Frank Capra which extended from the classic *Mr Deeds Goes to Town* (1936) to the tougher *Meet John Doe* (1941). The characters remained true to type and true to Cooper: men of integrity faced with

Top left: he was chosen to star in For Whom the Bell Tolls, *which led to his fourth Oscar nomination for his role as a Loyalist fighter in the Spanish Civil War. Top right: in 1941 Cooper had won an Oscar for* Sergeant York, *becoming an idol of an America recently plunged into World War II. Right: a typical stance from* The Real Glory *this was perhaps his most violent film. Centre top and bottom:* High Noon *won Cooper a second Oscar in 1952 for his intense portrayal of the lone and bitter sheriff*

that made the audience sit up and take notice.

Paramount signed him up and he worked non-stop. As the uncompromising lawman in *The Virginian* (1929) he followed the code of good versus bad, allowing no deviation in his search for justice. It was in this film that he coined that famous misquoted phrase 'when you call me that, smile!' Cooper believed that this was his best Western, although:

'I liked *The Plainsman*, the one I did for Cecil B. DeMille. But, of course, it was romanticized. Wild Bill Hickok, the character I played, wasn't really a very nice man.'

He then co-starred with Marlene Dietrich in *Morocco* (1930) but loathed Josef von Sternberg

himself in love with his co-star Patricia Neal, but Cooper's wife – being an ardent Catholic – would not give him a divorce. In 1951 the romance, a very discreet affair, was over. In the meantime Warners starred Cooper in action films such as *Task Force* (1949), a routine naval drama, because they felt that the public would not accept Cooper in his usual spotless-hero guise until the adverse publicity died down.

After a period in the doldrums, he won his second Oscar for his performance in *High Noon* (1952) which revitalized his screen career. He couldn't quite understand why: 'It was just a good story of the policeman who had to do a job and the townsfolk who were prepared to let him do it alone. But it was a good script and we

Left: Cooper urges an astonished Dana Andrews to fight in Ball of Fire *(1941). Below: Ten North Frederick (1958) showed fans an ageing Cooper. Bottom: The last film released before his death was* The Wreck of the Mary Deare *(1959) with Charlton Heston*

had a fine director, Fred Zinnemann. I really didn't see it as a psychological Western.'

In the last two years of his life he was surprised that he should be regarded as a Western hero, not having made many Westerns. He recalled with more affection films like *The Court-Martial of Billy Mitchell* (1955), about an American general brought before a judicial court for accusing the war department of criminal negligence, and *Ten North Frederick* (1958), where the members of a dead man's family look back on the events of his life. In both films Cooper played characters wrestling with the realities of contemporary life.

Before he died in 1961, he was awarded an honorary Oscar for his services to the film industry. As a screen actor, Cooper had the same fundamental idea as all the great stars:

'You have to go through the mill first. It's not good to become a big star with your first film. An actor has to have lived a little.'

Cooper lived a lot and died too soon.

MARGARET HINXMAN

the nauseous machinations of big business or big politics.

In 1941 Cooper won his first Oscar for his performance as the conscientious objector who becomes a war hero in *Sergeant York*, and in *Ball of Fire* (also 1941) he put his shy manner to fine use in a comedy role in which he played a meek professor researching slang who pursues a gangster's moll and finds himself in trouble.

The Fountainhead (1949), based on Ayn Rand's novel about an idealistic architect and his fight against big business, was a turning point in his private life. Married to a New York socialite Veronica Balfe since 1933, he found

Filmography

1923 Blind Justice. '25 The Thundering Herd; Wild Horse Mesa; The Lucky Horseshoe; The Vanishing American (GB: The Vanishing Race); The Eagle; Tricks; Lightnin' Wins (short). '26 Three Pals; The Enchanted Hill; Watch Your Wife; The Winning of Barbara Worth. '27 It; Children of Divorce; Arizona Bound; Wings; The Last Outlaw; Nevada. '28 Beau Sabreur; Doomsday; Legion of the Condemned; Half a Bride; The First Kiss; Lilac Time (GB: Love Never Dies); The Shopworn Angel. '29 Wolf Song; Betrayal; The Virginian. '30 Seven Days Leave/Medals; Only the Brave; Paramount on Parade; The Texan; A Man from Wyoming; The Spoilers; Morocco. '31 Fighting Caravans; City Streets; I Take This Woman; His Woman. '32 Make Me a Star (guest); Devil and the Deep; If I Had a Million; A Farewell to Arms; The Stolen Jools (GB: The Slippery Pearls) (guest) (short); Voice of Hollywood (guest) (short). '33 Today We Live; One Sunday Afternoon; Alice in Wonderland; Design for Living. '34 Operator 13 (GB: Spy 13); Now and Forever. '35 The Lives of a Bengal Lancer; Star Night at the Cocoanut Grove (guest) (short); The Wedding Night; Peter Ibbetson. '36 Desire; La Fiesta de Santa Barbara (guest) (short); Mr Deeds Goes to Town; Hollywood Boulevard (guest); The General Died at Dawn; The Plainsman. '37 Lest We Forget (guest) (short); Souls at Sea. '38 The Adventures of Marco Polo; Bluebeard's Eighth Wife; The Cowboy and the Lady. '39 Beau Geste; The Real Glory. '40 The Westerner; North West Mounted Police. '41 Meet John Doe; Sergeant York; Ball of Fire. '42 The Pride of the Yankees. '43 For Whom the Bell Tolls. '44 Memo for Joe (guest) (short); The Story of Dr Wassell; Casanova Brown. '45 Along Came Jones (+ prod); Saratoga Trunk (begun in '43). '46 Cloak and Dagger (final reel removed before release and never restored). '47 Variety Girl (guest); Unconquered. '48 Good Sam. '49 The Fountainhead; Snow Carnival (guest) (short); It's a Great Feeling (guest); Task Force. '50 Bright Leaf; Dallas; It's a Big Country. '51 You're in the Navy Now/USS Teakettle; Starlift (guest); Distant Drums. '52 High Noon; Springfield Rifle. '53 Return to Paradise; Blowing Wild. '54 Garden of Evil; Vera Cruz. '55 The Court-Martial of Billy Mitchell (GB: One Man Mutiny); Hollywood Mothers (guest) (short). '56 Friendly Persuasion. '57 Love in the Afternoon. '58 Ten North Frederick; Man of the West; The Hanging Tree. '59 Alias Jesse James (guest); They Came to Cordura; The Wreck of the Mary Deare. '61 The Naked Edge; The Real West (TV doc) (narr. only). '76 Hollywood on Trial (featured in doc. footage).

Kirk Douglas

Kirk Douglas' energy and magnetism dominate every picture he is in. He seems to challenge audiences with the question – is the hole in his jutting chin a beautifying dimple put there by the Almighty or the imprint of a hoodlum's toecap?

Casting a Giant Shadow

An aggressive vitality, a driving egotism – these are the distinctive qualities conveyed by Kirk Douglas, whose forcefulness repels some cinemagoers as much as it grips others. As an actor who has chosen his own roles since the early Fifties, run his own production company and (more recently) ventured into direction, he has favoured parts in which he can play the brazen individualist, the man out of step with the world around him. His most notable characters are intense, moody, powerful, often tragic – either they are crushed by a society that cannot tolerate them or they destroy themselves through a fatal flaw in their makeup. As the slave leader in *Spartacus* (1960), he is finally captured and crucified (though the real Spartacus died in battle); as the fanatical policeman in *Detective Story* (1951), he destroys his marriage when he cannot forgive his wife for once having had an abortion and effectively commits suicide by stopping a bullet fired by a crazed criminal.

No mercy
Occasionally in his films, others have fallen victim to an oppressive society while Douglas has been cast as a concerned observer. In the powerful *Paths of Glory* (1957), Douglas played a French officer in World War I who tries in vain to prevent four of his men, scapegoats for the failures of the high command, from being executed; a similar situation is given a 'black' twist in *Town Without Pity* (1961), in which Douglas portrays an American Major in World War II who successfully defends four GIs accused of rape by destroying the reputation of the German girl they attacked, driving her to suicide.

But more often Douglas' characters have

been the victims of their own aggression and ambition. The role that established his hard, ruthless image was that of Midge Kelly, the boxer in *Champion* (1949) who fights his way to the top, unscrupulously betraying his associates, and then dies from injuries sustained in the ring rather than accept defeat. Somewhat in the same vein was his newspaperman in *Ace in the Hole* (1951) who whips up the plight of a man trapped in a cave into a

Top: in Spartacus, *Kirk Douglas plays the gladiator who rebels and leads the slave revolt against the Romans. Above left:* Young Man With a Horn *(1950), based on the life of Twenties jazz musician Bix Beiderbeck, was one of Douglas' many biopics. Above: in* The Bad and the Beautiful *he played a film producer who makes his star (Lana Turner) fall in love with him so that she will give a powerful and passionate performance on the screen*

18

national story, delaying his rescue and causing the man's death.

In *The Bad and the Beautiful* (1952) Douglas brought a saving veneer of charm to the role of film producer Jonathan Shields who uses people but at the same time enables them to realize their own talents: a star (Lana Turner), a director (Barry Sullivan) and a writer (Dick Powell) are burned by their contact with him but at the end of the film are tempted to help him out when he needs them again.

Douglas was even intensely sympathetic in one of his favourite roles, that of the modern-day cowboy in *Lonely Are the Brave* (1962). Attempting to escape on horseback from the

law, he is finally killed crossing a highway by a truck carrying a load of toilet fittings. Douglas' characters court death: his dedicated military commander of *Cast a Giant Shadow* (1966) saves Israel from the Arabs but is senselessly killed by a sentry on his own side when he fails to answer a challenge in Hebrew, a language he does not understand. True to history, it is nevertheless the kind of ironical ending that seemingly delights Douglas.

A marked man

Pain and physical mutilation frequently shape and test the outlook of his screen characters. In *Man Without a Star* (1955) Douglas portrayed

The many faces of Kirk Douglas. Top left: the painter Vincent Van Gogh with Willemein (Jill Bennett) in Lust for Life. *Top: the northwest frontiersman in* The Big Sky. *Above left: the out-of-time cowboy in* Lonely Are the Brave. *Above: the faded film star with his director (Edward G. Robinson) in* Two Weeks in Another Town *(1962).*

Filmography
1946 The Strange Love of Martha Ivers. '47 I Walk Alone; Mourning Becomes Electra; Out of the Past (GB: Build My Gallows High). '48 The Walls of Jericho; My Dear Secretary; A Letter to Three Wives. '49 Champion. '50 Young Man With a Horn (GB: Young Man of Music); The Glass Menagerie. '51 Along the Great Divide; Ace in the Hole (USA retitling for TV: The Big Carnival); Detective Story; The Big Trees. '52 The Big Sky; The Bad and Beautiful. '53 The Story of Three Loves ep Equilibrium; The Juggler; Un Acte d'Amour (FR) (USA/GB: Act of Love). '54 Ulisse (IT) (USA/GB: Ulysses); 20,000 Leagues Under the Sea. '55 The Racers (GB: Such Men Are Dangerous); Man Without a Star; The Indian Fighter. '56 Lust for Life. '57 Top Secret Affair (GB: Their Secret Affair); Gunfight at the OK Corral; Paths of Glory. '58 The Vikings. '59 Last Train From Gun Hill; The Devil's Disciple. '60 Strangers When We Meet; Spartacus (+exec. prod). '61 The Last Sunset (+exec. prod); Town Without Pity. '62 Lonely Are the Brave; Two Weeks in Another Town; The Hook. '63 The List of Adrian Messenger; For Love or Money. '64 Seven Days in May. '65 In Harm's Way; The Heroes of Telemark (GB). '66 Cast a Giant Shadow; Paris, Brûle-t-il? (FR) (USA/GB: Is Paris Burning?). '67 The Way West; The War Wagon. '68 A Lovely Way to Die (GB: A Lovely Way to Go); The Brotherhood (+prod); French Lunch (short). '69 The Arrangement. '70 There Was A Crooked Man . . . '71 A Gunfight; La Luz del Fin del Mundo (USA-SP-LIECHTENSTEIN) (USA/GB: The Light at the Edge of the World); Catch Me a Spy (GB-FR): Summertree (prod. only). '73 Un Uomo da Rispettare (IT) (USA: The Master Tough/Hearts and Minds; GB: A Man to Respect; Scalawag (+dir) (USA-IT). '74 Cat and Mouse (GB) (USA retitling for TV: Mousey). '75 Posse (+dir); Once Is Not Enough/Jacqueline Susann's Once Is Not Enough. '77 Victory at Entebbe (shot as TV film but shown in cinemas); Holocaust 2000 (GB-IT) (USA: The Chosen). '78 The Fury. '79 The Villain (GB: Cactus Jack); Home Movies. '80 Saturn 3; The Final Countdown.

another cowboy fleeing the encroachment of civilization (represented by the enclosing of the range with barbed wire). In the film's most intense moment, Douglas rips off his shirt to explain his detestation of the wire, revealing the scars it has left on his body.

In the pioneering saga *The Big Sky* (1952), the Douglas character loses a finger in a sequence pitched for grotesque comedy by the director Howard Hawks. As Vincent Van Gogh in *Lust for Life* (1956), Douglas was thoroughly convincing (apart from the intractable prob-

lem of accent) and conveyed the torment that drove the painter to cut off his ear. As Einar in *The Vikings* (1958), a production of Douglas' Bryna company, he lost an eye to a hawk. In *Scalawag* (1973), Douglas directed himself as a one-legged pirate. Add such incidents as his self-imposed flogging by a black manservant in *The Way West* (1967) and the gruesome end of his dastardly villain, George Brougham, in *The List of Adrian Messenger* (1963) – flung onto the spikes of a concealed plough in place of his intended victim – and his career seems littered with instances of physical suffering that serve as a harsh, but often fitting, reward for the way his characters conduct themselves.

Born under a bad sign

'Virtue isn't photogenic', is the actor's avowed reason for portraying rogues. Even when his violent impulses have a conventional motivation, Douglas' characters have their grief compounded. In *Last Train From Gun Hill* (1959), he plays a marshal pursuing the murderers of his Indian wife. The principal killer turns out to be the son of his best friend.

In *Gunfight at the OK Corral* (1957), Douglas convincingly conveyed the self-disgust that possessed his alcoholic Doc Holliday, just as in *Lust for Life* he vividly rendered the mental anguish that drove Van Gogh to kill himself. More melodramatically, there were his characters in *The Last Sunset* (1961) and *In Harm's Way* (1965) who expiate their sins by inviting certain death in the dignified circumstances of, respectively, a gunfight undertaken with an empty gun and a suicide mission over Japanese waters in World War II.

Even Douglas' patriotic officer of *Seven Days in May* (1964) is afflicted with self-disgust. He reveals a military plot to overthrow the government but he detests being an informer and basically disapproves of the peace-mongering policies of a weak President that have prompted the conspiracy; he is also disturbed at having to recover from a socialite love letters that might be used to blackmail the leader of the conspirators.

Douglas has a reputation for being as forceful off-screen as on. 'I've always insisted on voicing my suggestions with directors,' he has declared, adding, 'The good ones have never objected.' Yet Anthony Mann left *Spartacus* after a disagreement with Douglas (Stanley Kubrick took over) and Robert Aldrich was unable to get on with his star and executive producer when working on *The Last Sunset*

(1961). Indeed, when Douglas made his directorial debut on *Scalawag*, he himself admitted: 'I've been *accused* of directing movies before but now I can be blamed.'

And blamed he was for *Scalawag*; he agreed in retrospect that he had mishandled the picture. However, functioning as director, producer and star of *Posse* (1975), he came up with a surprisingly accomplished and biting Western. He once again played a thwarted self-seeker, whose attempts to make political capital out of the capture of a notorious train-robber rebound on him when the badman lures the posse away and leaves him alone and ridiculed.

Douglas' efforts to play more relaxed parts in contemporary comedies like *Top Secret Affair* (1957) and *For Love or Money* (1963) have made him seem dull, though there was a virile humour to his period rogues of *The Devil's Disciple* (1959) and *The War Wagon* (1967). Douglas needed scope to bring feeling to his parts: the passion to paint he conveyed as no other Hollywood actor ever has in *Lust for Life*. Given a role which he could naturally invest with his own dedication and determination, he has shown himself to be a very considerable performer indeed. ALLEN EYLES

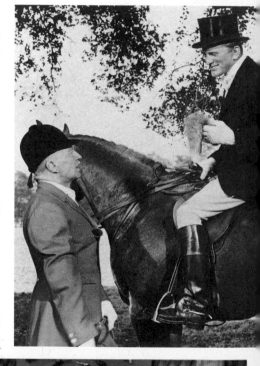

Above, far right: the master of disguise receives the tail for the winning ride from the Marquis of Gleneyre (Clive Brook) in The List of Adrian Messenger. *Right: the gunman hired to kill Taw Jackson (John Wayne) in* The War Wagon

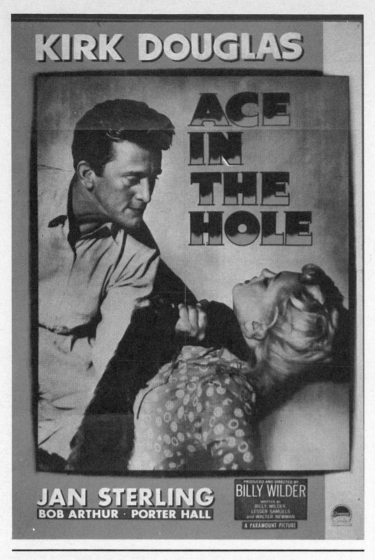

Directed by Billy Wilder, 1951
Prod co: Paramount. **prod:** Billy Wilder. **assoc prod:** William Schorr. **sc:** Billy Wilder, Lesser Samuels, Walter Newman. **photo:** Charles B. Lang Jr. **ed:** Doane Harrison, Arthur Schmidt. **art dir:** Hal Periera, Earl Hendrick. **mus:** Hugo Friedhofer. **song:** 'We're Coming Leo' by Ray Evans, Jay Livingston. **sd:** John Cope, Harold Lewis. **ass dir:** C. C. Coleman Jr. **r/t:** 111 minutes.
Cast: Kirk Douglas (*Chuck Tatum*), Jan Sterling (*Lorraine*), Bob Arthur (*Herbie Cook*), Porter Hall (*Jacob Q. Boot*), Frank Cady (*Mr Federber*), Richard Benedict (*Leo Minosa*), Ray Teal (*sheriff*), Lewis Martin (*McCardle*), John Berkes (*Papa Minosa*), Frances Domingues (*Mama Minosa*), Gene Evans (*deputy sheriff*), Frank Jaquett (*Smollett*), Harry Harvey (*Dr Hilton*), Bob Bumpas (*radio announcer*), Geraldine Hall (*Mrs Federber*), Richard Gaines (*Nagel*).

Billy Wilder's work is characterized by the acidity and virulence with which it represents various facets of the American way of life, but none of his films is so blackly ferocious as *Ace in the Hole*, a bitter, corrosive portrait of gutter journalism, public voyeurism and blatant official corruption. Like Robert Aldrich's *Kiss Me Deadly* (1955) the film can be read as a harsh critique of the whole 'hard-boiled' Hollywood tradition. It can also be seen as going still further and, long before the under-rated *Fedora* (1978), attacking a whole tradition of cinema, a typically American tradition – the cinema of spectacle.

Wilder's films are packed with hard-boiled Americans, such as Walter Neff in *Double Indemnity* (1944), Don Birnam in *The Lost Weekend* (1945) and Joe Gillis in *Sunset Boulevard* (1950), but for sheer unmitigated avarice and naked ambition Chuck Tatum has no equal, except perhaps Walter Matthau's Willie Gingrich in *The Fortune Cookie* (1966). However, Wilder is even more uncompromising in his depiction of the grasping and hypocritical society surrounding Tatum, of which the reporter is but an extreme personification. The huge crowds which gather at the scene of the accident, the carnival atmosphere surrounding the whole event, all this recalls the vision of the monstrous mob in Nathanael West's novel *The Day of the Locust*. Tatum, atop the mountain marshalling the multitudes, resembles

nothing less than the director of some cinematic epic, the ultimate *metteur-en-scène*.

Ace in the Hole demonstrates how the forces of show business and commercialism cater to the public's basest instincts by exploiting disaster. Just as in *Sunset Boulevard*, in which the Hollywood audience is characterized as a mob of 'heartless so-and-so's' feeding off an ageing film star's personal tragedies, so here the holidaying crowds' relationship with Leo's situation is represented as essentially vampiric. It is their appetite for sensation which makes possible the whole 'rescue' charade that prolongs Leo's agony. The Mountain of the Seven Vultures under which Leo is trapped becomes the Mountain of the Seven Thousand Vultures as crowds of people come to 'gorge' off a private tragedy and stare at a 'real-life drama' as if it were a mere series of images on a cinema or TV screen. The way in which Wilder organizes this 'audience' and its physical relationship to the spectacle actually turns the site into the equivalent of a drive-in cinema, as Adrian Turner and Neil Sinyard point out in their book *Journey Down Sunset Boulevard*:

'The cars line up in orderly rows, just as people sit in theatres, their attention focused on the mountain. The spatial relationship between the viewer and the screen is precisely echoed, and to the thousands of spectators the drama on the mountain must resemble a movie. They have to purchase a ticket (at an ever-increasing price . . .) to get a decent view, and Lorraine's trading post becomes the traditional popcorn kiosk, providing refreshments during the ''intervals'' when nothing is happening.'

When Leo dies, the crowds evaporate: within minutes the place is

deserted, like an empty cinema strewn with litter. Once the spectacle is over, no-one wants to listen to Tatum or hear his uncomfortable words.

Hardly surprisingly for a film which attacks so many cherished American totems, not to mention the audience itself, *Ace in the Hole* was a financial disaster; indeed, it seemed to manifest such an utter and complete disregard for the usual commercial, box-office values as to be actively courting the dubious distinction of becoming a *film maudit*.

Paramount appeared not to know what to do with a film which aroused so much hostility. They decided to change the title to *The Big Carnival*, thereby ironically publicizing the very phenomenon which the film attacked so vehemently. In the wake of official attempts to stop the film being shown in countries that harboured American interests, it was banned in Singapore on the grounds that it portrayed a facet of American life that 'might be misunderstood'. In Hollywood it was said that the film, Wilder's first after his break with his long-time collaborator Charles Brackett, proved, as the critic Axel Madsen put it, that 'Wilder had no heart and less taste'. Madsen continued:

'He was a compassionless cynic whose excess of contempt for humanity had only been controlled by the elegant and wise old Brackett.'

This judgment would be proved radically wrong by Wilder's later works, such as *The Private Life of Sherlock Holmes* (1970) and *Avanti!* (1972) which testify to Wilder's strongly Romantic streak.

JULIAN PETLEY

Below: Billy Wilder discusses a scene with Richard Benedict who plays Leo Minosa, the trapped man

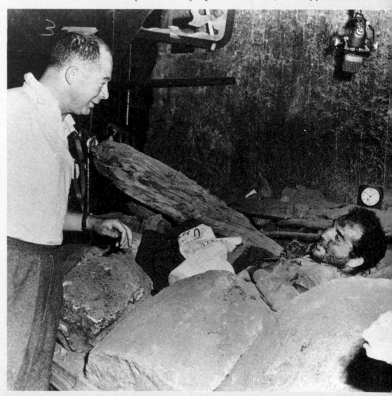

In the Sixties and Seventies Clint Eastwood seemed too good to be true. He transformed himself overnight from a smiling cowboy in a TV series into a deadly, inscrutable fantasy hero idolized by millions. Whatever he touched turned to gold, and so the biggest star in the world also became a highly successful director – but what does the future hold now for Clint?

The Beguiler

There was an unexpected box-office lapse in the summer of 1980 – *Bronco Billy* didn't do very well. It should have been reliable business with Clint Eastwood's brushed leather face beneath a dashing white cowboy hat. He was surrounded by the people from previous hits. His deadpan reaction to mishap was funny, without destroying his authority. *Bronco Billy* had the air of a happy summer movie, as full of fights, laughs and male self-congratulation as *Every Which Way But Loose* (1978), the Eastwood Christmas film of two years before and a hit beyond anyone's wildest dreams. The latter was a departure: it was the first Eastwood film to try comedy action, as if to say, 'Look, this guy is 48, and he can't go around stomping on everyone for much longer'. It gave Clint an orang-utan to tuck under one arm, while the other retained its gentlemanly hold on Sondra Locke. The successful formula was repeated with *Any Which Way You Can* (1980), but *Bronco Billy* had been the first film to raise the possibility that Eastwood is not infallible.

The Man With No Failures
For 16 years, he had enjoyed unrivalled success. Not every picture triumphed – one of the best, *The Beguiled* (1971), was too sardonic to please his following – but they all went about their business of entertaining large audiences. Eastwood didn't win much review space, and when he did it was because critics like Pauline Kael were alarmed by what they felt lay beneath the surface of violent cop movies like *Dirty Harry* (1971). Nevertheless, since 1964, about twenty Eastwood pictures had prospered. And if Eastwood was quiet, unstarry and inclined to stay at home at Carmel,

California, rather than play the talk shows, still he had gone from being actor to star to director and boss of his own company, Malpaso. That tight-knit operation made all his Seventies pictures – and took big profits from them.

No-one has ever begrudged him this glory. He handles himself gracefully, especially because he has acted on the notion that turning out pleasant movies is not that difficult. His pictures are not expensive and they never strive after the difficult or the pretentious. Twenty years earlier he was a good-looking Californian kid with hair like James Dean's and swimming-pool blue eyes. He would look better as he matured, but if it hadn't been for the shyness of someone who had reached six foot by the age of 13, he might have carried showbiz on the strength of beauty alone. Not since Gary Cooper had an American male in pictures had it in his power to stop the breath

Above: death in the desert for adversaries of the Man With No Name – Eastwood in For a Few Dollars More *(and right). Below left: Clint learns to ballroom dance at the Universal talent school around 1955. His partner was Italian actress Gia Scala*

of men and women in the audience alike. No matter how tough the roles, the skin, the eyes and the very soft voice have hinted at a Malibu Apollo.

For a very few dollars . . .
He was born in San Francisco in 1930. The family was poor and Clint went from high school to manual labour, laying down the basis for that lean body. He was an army swimming instructor at Ford Ord, and then he started to study business at Los Angeles College. But physique and looks earned him offers from Universal – a starting contract at $75 a week. In 1955, he got a couple of walk-on parts in movies, including *Francis in the Navy*, starring Donald O'Connor and a talking mule.

Those were tough days. Clint looked too healthy and he spoke too clearly to fit the Brando style. He was in and out of work, taking acting classes by night and doing labouring jobs in the day. The body got harder, but he didn't put much faith in lessons or theory:

'The basic fundamental of learning acting is to know yourself, know what you can do. That's one big advantage of doing a series, if you can. You get to see yourself a lot, get to see what you can do wrong or right.'

His television series was *Rawhide*, and the role of Rowdy Yates was no more than an outline that a young actor could inhabit in front of the camera. Over two hundred episodes in seven seasons provided Eastwood with

'spaghetti' Western had proved cold and greasy the actor would have been thrown out in the garbage.

Leone and the language of death

However, the film was a huge, international hit that changed Eastwood's life and, in the Man With No Name, created a role model that still works in TV advertising. The film was made by Sergio Leone, whose English was as limited as Clint's Italian. But they got on well and understood that the image of a laconic but lethal man musing on a cheroot until blazing guns appeared from beneath his serape, could be sensational.

The costume was bought by Eastwood in America. He conceived the character, and he rewrote or cut many of his lines. *A Fistful of Dollars* and its sequels – *Per Qualche Dollaro in Più* (1966, *For a Few Dollars More*) and *Il Buono, il Brutto, il Cattivo* (1967, *The Good, the Bad and the Ugly*) – were full of pregnant pauses just because of the language problem on set, but that only stimulated Leone's visual imagination and allowed Clint to become an awesome assassin, above words, a face always gazing into the sun so that the eyes seemed to be glints of some rare and impervious metal. A ruthless, implacable honour grew around the silence and the eyes that would not look away. The movies were like mescal dreams, poised wonderfully between suspense and absurdity.

In later years, Clint was often willing to have his super-hero outsmarted – by women, an elderly Indian and that orang-utan. But that's not new. Leone's films were very violent, and they played the action straight – if that's the way you wanted to read it. Yet the exaggerated compositions, the mannered acting and the feeling of time oozing out as slowly as ketchup all suggested a satiric attitude on the part of the director and his star.

The *Dollars* trilogy kept Clint occupied in the

that necessary view of himself. Now he is one of few screen stars with the instinctive assurance of knowing how a scene should be filmed. His face, his minimal reactions and his timing are a style such as Cooper and Bogart had possessed before him.

Even on *Rawhide* he was asking to direct some episodes. Eric Fleming, the lead star on the show, had no problems with Clint's ambitions. But CBS and the unions were very touchy and they restricted him to trailers. Still, it is a mark of Eastwood's love of movies that the urge to make them came early, apparently on a day when a stampede scene was being shot from a safe distance and Clint wondered why he couldn't carry a camera on horseback into the herd.

He could have been numbered with James Arness, Robert Horton or, indeed, Eric Fleming – stars in Western series who retired, got trapped in television, or in the case of Fleming, died in 1966 on the slide. Clint proved his initiative with what seemed an affront to Hollywood tradition. He went to Spain to make a Western for an Italian director. It was called *Per un Pugno di Dollari* (1964, *A Fistful of Dollars*) and he did it for $15,000: if the

mid-Sixties. When he returned to America, he set about making this new kind of Western at home: *Hang 'Em High* (1968), *Two Mules for Sister Sara* (1970), *Joe Kidd* (1972) and *High Plains Drifter* (1973) are all in the same vein. The lesson that he had learned was that the outsider hero suited him – not just a nameless figure, but a man without known allegiances. In 1968, for the first time, he teamed up with Don Siegel, a director of twenty years hard-earned experience and an expert story-teller with a predilection for toughness. Siegel had always found Hollywood stars squeamish when asked to be mean, but Clint was different:

'Eastwood has an absolute fixation as an anti-hero. It's his credo in life and in all the films that he's done so far . . . I've never worked with an actor who was less conscious of his good image.'

Coogan's Bluff – about an Arizona cop who comes on a manhunt to New York – isn't quite that heartless, but it did exploit the novelty of that handsome face snarling with hostility, of the Eastwood hero coolly laying any woman around. Siegel would be as important to Eastwood as Leone, but there were a few years of hesitation before the new partnership clicked. Eastwood was overshadowed by Richard Burton in Brian Hutton's *Where Eagles Dare* (1968) and by Lee Marvin in Joshua Logan's *Paint Your Wagon* (1969).

Play dirty for Siegel

The year in which he emerged as a Hollywood giant was 1971. For Siegel he acted in *The Beguiled*, about a fugitive in the American Civil War taken in by a household of women who take sweet vengeance on his complacent stud attitudes by amputating his injured leg. Then he directed his first film, *Play Misty for Me*, a slick thriller about a disc jockey who is haunted and nearly killed by a woman who

Right: Eastwood's directorial debut starred him as DJ Dave Garland who is plagued by the psychopathic woman (Jessica Walter) who asks him to Play Misty for Me

Above: Eastwood as a ghost about to exact explosive revenge in High Plains Drifter. *Above right: as a cop forced to run* The Gauntlet *with a hooker (regular co-star Sondra Locke) – love blossoms, naturally. Clint directed both box-office successes*

phones up with the request of the title. In both these pictures Clint was making himself the victim of women, and surely that owed itself to the good humour of a happily married man lusted after by so many strangers.

Dirty Harry, though, was the major event of 1971, and the most controversial film he has ever made. Siegel's direction guaranteed its impact, but the subject went beyond mere entertainment. Dirty Harry Callahan is a San Francisco cop with an old-fashioned belief in the law and the will that must enforce it. The film is in two parts: first Harry tracks down a loathsome killer, a nasty mixture of spoiled kid

psychopath and glib hippy; but then bureaucracy and the technicalities of the law let the killer go free whereupon Harry makes a private war on him, eliminating him with prejudice and then tossing away his police badge in disgust.

Some people felt that the picture encouraged vigilante fascism, that it was urging less liberal law-and-order programmes (Eastwood had backed Nixon in 1968). But the picture is more the manifestation of a very independent, romantic morality that shows in the star's aversion to publicity, extravagance and institutions:

'We, as Americans, went to Nuremberg and convicted people who committed certain crimes because they didn't adhere to a higher morality; we convicted them on that basis – and they shouldn't have listened to the law of the land or their leaders at that time. They should have listened to the true morality.'

Softening the blows

It seems likely that he was affected by complaints about the violence in *Dirty Harry* and its successors, *Magnum Force* (1973), *The Enforcer* (1976) and *The Gauntlet* (1977). His anti-hero has mellowed to become a more relaxed, more amused and marginally less robust observer. That was the process of tolerance that worked so well in *The Outlaw Josey Wales* (1976), in which a righteous moral anger softens with time to become aware of foibles, frailty and humour. In many ways it is his most adventurous picture, a sign of the kindness he is often too shy or laid back to reveal.

Nor would anyone have expected *Breezy* (1973) from Eastwood. With William Holden and Kay Lenz, that was the story of a September-May romance, shamelessly sentimental but touching, solidly grounded and well acted. For Clint it was about a man who 'rediscovers life through the eyes of this young girl'. It was the first hint that he might be fearful of growing older, and it could have been a prelude to his own romantic interest in Sondra Locke. He resists confessions or the gossip press, but for some time he has worked with the younger, blonde actress who has not

really acted for anyone but Eastwood (though the failure of *Bronco Billy* apparently threatened their relationship).

He is over fifty now, with reason to wonder about his future. His face has begun to look strained; in the rather dull *Escape From Alcatraz* (1979) there was evidence of youth withering away. Gary Cooper made *High Noon* (1952) when he was 51, after several years of indecision. And at about the same age John Wayne yielded to paternal roles in *The Searchers* (1956) and *Rio Bravo* (1959). It may be that Eastwood's greatest test lies ahead. Can he find and prove himself in older parts? Is he inventive enough to discover a fresh character, or will his career wane? He might settle for directing and for running his own company, but if you have been as beautiful as Clint Eastwood, and as adored, it may be very hard to give up being looked at.

DAVID THOMSON

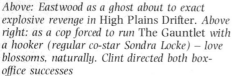

Filmography
1955 Revenge of the Creature; Lady Godiva (GB: Lady Godiva of Coventry); Francis in the Navy; Tarantula; Never Say Goodbye. **'56** Star in the Dust; The First Travelling Saleslady. **'57** Escapade in Japan. **'58** Lafayette Escadrille (GB: Hell Bent for Glory); Ambush at Cimarron Pass. **'64** Per un Pugno di Dollari (IT-GER-SP) (USA/GB: A Fistful of Dollars). **'66** Per Qualche Dollaro in Più (IT-GER-SP) (USA/GB: For a Few Dollars More). **'67** Il Buono, il Brutto, il Cattivo (IT-GER-SP) (USA/GB: The Good, the Bad and the Ugly); Le Streghe *ep* Una Sera Come le Altre (IT-FR) (USA: The Witches *ep* A Night Like Any Other). **'68** Hang 'Em High; Coogan's Bluff; Where Eagles Dare (GB). **'69** Paint Your Wagon. **'70** Gold Fever (doc. short) (appearance as himself); Two Mules for Sister Sara; Kelly's Heroes (USA-YUG). **'71** The Beguiled; Play Misty for Me (+dir); Dirty Harry. **'72** Joe Kidd. **'73** High Plains Drifter (+dir); Breezy (dir. only); Magnum Force. **'74** Thunderbolt and Lightfoot. **'75** The Eiger Sanction (+dir). **'76** The Outlaw Josey Wales (+dir); The Enforcer. **'77** The Gauntlet (+dir). **'78** Every Which Way But Loose. **'79** Escape From Alcatraz. **'80** Bronco Billy (+dir); Any Which Way You Can.

Heston's Heroes

From Moses to Michelangelo, Charlton Heston has played some memorable parts in movie history. But behind the monumental façade of the epic hero is a man of concern and sensitivity – a perfectionist of the craft of cinema acting

Charlton Heston, Hollywood's greatest epic hero, is also perhaps Hollywood's most under-rated actor. Such critical neglect stems in the main from his close association with epic films – a genre which has been traditionally under-valued by critics who, when reviewing them, all seem to become historical experts more concerned to list factual inaccuracies than to appreciate the visual power and mythic force of the films.

In all Heston's epics, he has been one of their greatest strengths. Towering in height, massive of frame, granite-hard and steel-thewed, Heston immediately elicits such adjectives as 'rugged', 'craggy', 'virile'. He stands tall and solid like one of the buttes in John Ford's beloved Monument Valley or the carved images of American Presidents at Mount Rushmore. His face is not a face of this century. The keen eyes, the strong jaw, the wide mouth, the broken nose, are the features of a medieval warrior-hero; his whole being is a living echo of heroic sagas and *chansons de geste*. It is a fitting appearance for an actor who, with total conviction and considerable skill, has conveyed such qualities as chivalry, duty, honour, courage and faith – the keystones of an age less sophisticated and less cynical than our own, yet undoubtedly more forceful, more direct and in some ways more appealing.

Critics have been deceived by his sheer size into thinking that he cannot be an actor. But he is both actor and a star. He has the presence, the charisma and the luminous quality of a

star; but he also has the dedication, the sensitivity and the intelligence of a great actor. His commitment to the acting profession shines through the journals that he kept from 1956 to 1976, and published in 1978 as *The Actor's Life*. These candid and remarkably illuminating journals reveal the man behind the image. He emerges as a devoted and highly principled actor, working hard at his craft, seeking always to improve, driving himself, testing himself, returning regularly to the stage and to his first love – Shakespeare – to maintain his links with the classical theatre. And yet he is not one of those actors who regard the stage as innately superior to film, as his passionate involvement in film-making proves.

A former President of the Screen Actors' Guild and Chairman of the American Film Institute, he has fought for projects he believed

Left: Heston in his award-winning role as Judah Ben-Hur. Below: a rare shot of Heston in tie and jacket, in Dark City, *one of the earliest films he made*

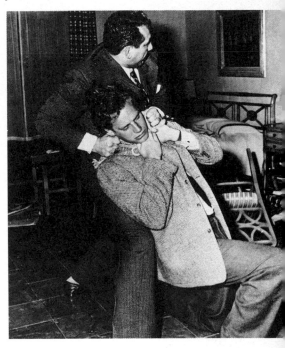

in, devoting years of his life to setting up such films as *The War Lord* (1965). When working on *Major Dundee* (1965) he handed back part of his salary to Columbia to pay for extra shooting which the director wanted and the company did not. More remarkably still, he took comparatively uninteresting roles in *The Big Country* and *Touch of Evil* (both 1958) for the experience of working with their directors, William Wyler and Orson Welles. He has of course had his failures: his bids to extend his range by playing comedy – *The Private War of Major Benson* (1955), *The Pigeon That Took Rome* (1962) – demonstrated conclusively that comedy is not his forte. In another carefully nurtured project he directed and played Mark Antony in a film of Shakespeare's *Antony and Cleopatra* (1972): the result was undistinguished. But always they are honourable failures.

It was both Heston's and Hollywood's good fortune that he was around and at the height of his powers when the industry turned in the Fifties and Sixties to large-scale epics in the hope of winning back audiences who were

being lost to television. Epic films need epic heroes – stars who do not just look the part but who also act the part. No one has equalled Heston in conveying the integrity, the intensity or the mystique of the true epic hero. Those qualities were already apparent to filmmaker David Bradley who cast Heston – then only twenty five – as Mark Antony in a 16mm film version of *Julius Caesar*, made in 1949 and shown in 1950.

A television appearance as Mr Rochester in *Jane Eyre* won Heston a film contract with producer Hal Wallis, then releasing through Paramount. He made his professional debut in a tough urban thriller, William Dieterle's *Dark City* (1950), a film which demonstrated how uncomfortable and out of place he looked in a suit and tie. Thereafter Paramount cast him in a series of routine action films such as *Pony Express*, *Arrowhead* (both 1953), *Secret of the Incas* (1954) and *The Far Horizons* (1955); during this period his career marked time. There were, however, two films in this period which hinted at his particular qualities: in Byron Haskin's *The Naked Jungle* (1954) he was perfectly cast as a defiant Amazonian planter battling against an army of soldier ants which threatened to devour his plantation. In Henry Levin's *The President's Lady* (1953) he played the legendary American President, General Andrew Jackson, 'Old Hickory'. Although the film, as its title suggests, was essentially a love story, Heston imbued his Jackson with mythic stature – so much so that he repeated the role in Anthony Quinn's disastrous 1958 remake of Cecil B. DeMille's *The Buccaneer*. Heston was one of the film's few saving graces.

The real breakthrough came when the shrewd old maestro DeMille cast him as Moses

Top left: El Cid does battle with the Moorish enemy. Above left: Heston in another spot of trouble, this time – with Senta Berger – in a scene from Major Dundee. *Above right: Heston, Ava Gardner and David Niven filming* 55 Days at Peking

in *The Ten Commandments* (1956). It was to be DeMille's last film, the triumphant summation of his remarkable career, and showed that he had lost none of his power or cunning in blending spectacle, sex, sadism and religiosity into a box-office blockbuster. Despite the visual power of sequences like the parting of the Red Sea and the destruction of the Golden Calf, the film's centre and focus was the figure of Moses. Heston was magnificent in the part: he transformed himself during its course from noble, commanding warrior-prince into Old Testament prophet – greying, bearded, determined and exuding a genuine apocalyptic splendour. His success in the part led him to become irrevocably associated with epic films.

The list of parts he was offered but which, for one reason or another, he did not accept, includes Darius the Great, Charlemagne, William the Conqueror, Oliver Cromwell, Hernan Cortes and General Custer. Nevertheless it was an epic role – the title part in *Ben-Hur* (1959) – that won him an Academy Award for best actor. William Wyler's film, with its impressive script by uncredited Christopher Fry, concentrates on the dichotomy between the totalitarian power of the Roman Empire and heroic individualism, embodied in an earnest Jewish nobleman, Judah Ben-Hur. The conflict is resolved in one of the cinema's most exciting action sequences: the climactic chariot race in which Ben-Hur bests Messala (Stephen Boyd),

the chief representative of ruthless Roman Imperialism.

In the Sixties Heston went on to star in three of the decade's best epics: Anthony Mann's *El Cid* (1961), Franklin Schaffner's *The War Lord* (1965) and Basil Dearden's *Khartoum* (1966). *El Cid*, the supreme vindication of the epic film, is stunningly handsome in its evocation of the Middle Ages, as seen through the eyes and verses of the troubadours. All noble qualities are epitomized in Rodrigo Diaz de Bivar, the legendary Spanish liberator 'El Cid', and as played by Charlton Heston he was truly 'the best and purest knight of all'. His death and apotheosis are charged with mythopoeic potency.

A Dark Age world of savagery and superstition is the equally powerful setting for *The War Lord* in which Heston plays the stern and formidable Norman war-lord Chrysagon, who abducts a Frisian village girl on her wedding night, only to fall in love with her and later defend her and his bleak, marshland stronghold against ferocious attacks. At the end, mortally wounded, he rides off into the mist, becoming like King Arthur 'the once and future king'.

Khartoum resoundingly demonstrated the subtlety and skill of Heston's art. For in this film he played a totally different sort of epic hero, General Gordon, the Empire's visionary leader who died resisting the forces of the Mahdi at Khartoum. With clipped English accent, monumental serenity of manner and inspirational conviction, Heston became the man who, armed with only a swagger stick, had led the armies of the Emperor of China to victory over the Taiping rebels. His achievement is emphasized by the fact that he com-

Above: more blood and pain in the medieval melodrama The War Lord. *Above right: with Genevieve Bujold in* Earthquake, *an example of Heston's recent switch from the epic to the more popular disaster movie. Left: strange emotional encounter in* Planet of the Apes. *Below: a brutal end for the solitary cowboy* Will Penny

pletely outplayed Laurence Olivier, whose Mahdi was a caricatured stage-black man, an uneasy mixture of Othello and Al Jolson.

Between these roles he played a US Marine major in a spectacular re-creation of the siege of the European legations in Peking by the Boxer rebels – *55 Days at Peking* (1963) – and John the Baptist in George Stevens' commercially disastrous *The Greatest Story Ever Told* (1965). In Carol Reed's *The Agony and the Ecstasy* (1965) – a misguided attempt to turn Michelangelo into an epic hero of art – Heston was miscast as the painter who, in reality short, ugly and neurotic, was his antithesis. And the glory was anyway stolen by Rex Harrison who played the engagingly raffish Pope Julius II.

Heston next demonstrated his versatility by lending his heroic stature to two of the Sixties' most notable westerns. Sam Peckinpah's *Major Dundee* (1965) remains (despite studio cutting) a complex meditation on the nature and identity of the United States, with Heston outstanding as the inflexible Puritan moralist Major Amos Dundee who, while pursuing an Apache war band in Mexico, experiences his own crisis of identity. Heston was equally impressive in a very different part – the rootless, illiterate, middle-aged cowboy in Tom Gries' much-praised *Will Penny* (1967) – achieving moments of deep pathos in the scenes with the young woman and her son whom Will befriends.

His particular gifts were also an asset to two science-fiction classics. In Franklin Schaffner's allegorical *Planet of the Apes* (1967) Heston was the marooned astronaut, while in Boris Sagal's underrated *The Omega Man* (1971) Heston was literally the last man on earth, a titanic Captain America figure waging a lone crusade against zombie mutations.

By the Seventies the vogue for historical epics had passed, and in their place the disaster movie held sway. Heston was an obvious choice to represent the human spirit struggling against cataclysm on land and sea and in the air. As such he fought his way through *Earthquake* (1974), *Skyjacked* (1972), *Airport 1975* (1974), *Gray Lady Down* (1978) and *Two-Minute Warning* (1976). Yet in all these films, in contrast to the historical epics, the emphasis was entirely on the spectacle. Plots were superficial, characterization minimal. However, even if Heston never again dons chain mail or unsheathes his broadsword, his contribution to the epic film has been potent and enormous. The legacy of the man who gave us Moses, Gordon and El Cid will certainly endure.

JEFFREY RICHARDS

Filmography
1941 Peer Gynt (semi-professional; commercial version shown '65). **'50** Julius Caesar (semi-professional); Dark City. **'51** The Greatest Show on Earth. **'52** The Savage; Ruby Gentry. **'53** Pony Express; The President's Lady; Arrowhead; Bad for Each Other. **'54** The Naked Jungle; Secret of the Incas. **'55** The Far Horizons; The Private War of Major Benson; Lucy Gallant. **'56** The Ten Commandments; Three Violent People/The Maverick. **'58** Touch of Evil; The Big Country; The Buccaneer. **'59** The Wreck of the Mary Deare (USA-GB); Ben-Hur. **'61** El Cid (USA-IT). **'62** The Pigeon That Took Rome. **'63** Diamond Head; 55 Days at Peking; The Five Cities of June (narr. only) (short). **'65** The Greatest Story Ever Told; Major Dundee; The Agony and the Ecstasy; The War Lord. **'66** Khartoum (GB). **'67** Planet of the Apes; Will Penny; The Battle Horns (GB: Counterpoint). **'69** Number One; Rowan and Martin at the Movies (narr. only) (short); The Heart of Variety (narr. only) (short). **'70** Beneath the Planet of the Apes; King: A Filmed Record . . . Montgomery to Memphis (co-narr. only) (doc) (retitling for TV: Martin Luther King); The Festival Game (narr. only) (short); The Hawaiians (GB: Master of the Islands); Julius Caesar (GB). **'71** The Omega Man. **'72** The Call of the Wild (GB-GER-SP-IT-FR); Antony and Cleopatra (+dir.+sc.) (SWIT-SP-GB); Skyjacked. **'73** Soylent Green; The Three Musketeers: The Queen's Diamonds (GB). **'74** Airport 1975; Earthquake. **'75** The Four Musketeers: The Revenge of Milady (PAN-SP); Won Ton Ton, the Dog That Saved Hollywood (guest). **'76** The Last Hard Men; Midway (GB: Battle of Midway); Two-Minute Warning; America at the Movies (narr. only) (doc). **'77** The Prince and the Pauper (PAN) (USA: Crossed Swords). **'78** Gray Lady Down. **'80** Mountain Men.

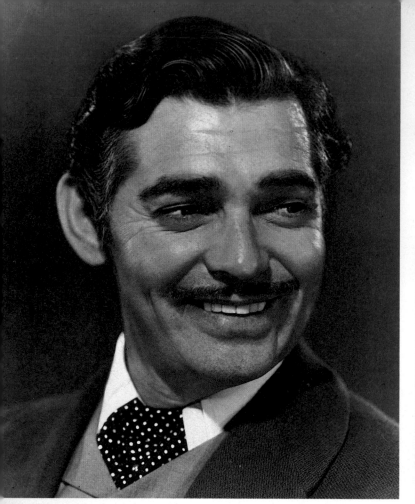

The Clark Gable Story

There was no nonsense with Gable. He was rough, tough and ready for anything. And when it came to women . . . well, frankly, he didn't give a damn. But who would have guessed that the King of Hollywood owed his early breaks as an actor to the care and encouragement of the women who wooed him?

When the age of talking pictures dawned in Hollywood, the two greatest romantic male stars of the silent era – Wallace Reid and Rudolph Valentino – were already a memory. Douglas Fairbanks Sr was ageing fast; so was Richard Barthelmess; and that other cavalier, John Gilbert, was in decline. The kings of the silents were all dead or dying. It was time to push the young princes forward and cry out 'Long live the King!'

The most promising heir apparent, ignored at first because he had protruding ears, became the public's choice for King. Twelve Clark Gable pictures were released during 1931, and there was little doubt that MGM, the studio that made most of them, was grooming him for stardom. In the second of those films, *Dance, Fools, Dance*, Gable played a brutal gangster giving Joan Crawford a bad time, and in his seventh role that year, in *A Free Soul*, he beat up Norma Shearer. In the silent days he would have been an out-and-out villain, but the film heroines of the Thirties were showing masochistic tastes, and thought of rugs as something not just to be walked on but dragged over.

William Clark Gable was born in Cadiz, Ohio, on February 1, 1901, the only child of farmer and oil-driller William H. Gable and his wife Adeline. His mother died when he was just seven months old, and his grandparents looked after him for two years until his father married again. William Jr's stepmother, Jennie Dunlap, was the best thing that could ever have happened to him; always a rough diamond, he learned from her the strength of tenderness. He worshipped her.

When young Gable finished his sophomore year at high school, he wanted to go to Akron with an older friend and work in a tyre factory, and his stepmother persuaded her husband to let the boy go. All through his life, women (usually older ones) put him on the right track and helped him forward. It was in Akron that he saw his first stage play, and he was entranced. He went backstage afterwards and got an unpaid job after factory hours as a call boy at the theatre, and was even sometimes given a few small parts with lines.

Gable was hooked. Not even when his stepmother died and his father compelled him to work with him in the Oklahoma oil fields could he forget the magic of the theatre. When he was 21 his grandfather gave him $300 and Gable took off for Kansas City, where he joined a company known as the Jewell Players.

The image everyone associates with Gable is such a virile one, and he played so many cowboys, reporters, oil-men, truckdrivers, auto-racers, boxers and soldiers in his time that he never had any trouble convincing his audiences and fans that he was anything but a hard-working male with square ideas. Certainly no-one would have guessed that at an early age he had drunk of theatre wine and really had little interest outside the stage. He was eager to learn more of the show world, and again it was the women he met who helped him. Among them was Franz Dorfler, an aspiring young actress who took him home to her parents when his stock company failed in Oregon, and saw to it that he was looked after. He marked time in Portland where he was variously employed, first by a newspaper and then a telephone company, until he got a job with an acting group. It was headed by actress and stage director Josephine Dillon, 14 years his senior, who was aware of what he had to offer as an actor and helped him refine his talents. She took him with her to Hollywood, where, on December 13, 1924, they were married.

Gable learned more about the craft of acting from her than he did from anybody else. She taught him physical grace so that he did not move like an oil-rigger; his deportment, both on and off stage, was exemplary. She bought him clothes, took him to a dentist so that he could smile unashamedly, showing off the deep dimples at the sides of his mouth, and persuaded him to drop the name 'William', and call himself Clark Gable. She also got him his first roles in films – mostly as an extra, though he did receive his first screen credit when he played Alice Joyce's brother in *White Man* (1924), and also had a bit part in *The Plastic Age* (1925), with Clara Bow.

Gable was aware that he needed more finesse as an actor and returned to the stage. He played juvenile for Lionel Barrymore in a production of *The Copperhead*. Then, separated from his wife, he let the ladies of the theatre take turns sponsoring him. Jane Cowl took him on as a spear-carrier in her production of *Romeo and Juliet*; Pauline Frederick cast him as the public prosecutor in her revival of *Madame X*, and as a nightclub owner in *Lucky Sam McCarver*. Gable often accompanied Miss Frederick socially; she bought him a new suit and paid for the further expensive dental work he needed. Apart from acting he had other duties to perform, as he grumpily explained, 'Miss Frederick is forever complaining she has a sore back. She likes me to rub it for her.'

After other minor roles he made his debut on the Broadway stage on September 7, 1928, in *Machinal*, playing the star's lover and attracting very good notices. On tour with another play in Texas, he met Mrs Ria Langham, a Houston socialite and several times a divorcee. She was very wealthy, and she liked what she saw when she looked at Clark Gable and followed him back to New York. Like others before her, she took him on as a 'special project'. Josephine Dillon had given him the essentials, but Mrs Langham, 17 years older than Gable and blessed with social contacts, gave him the polishing touches. She took him to the best tailor, the best bootery, the best barber, the best everything. He developed manners, confidence and ease. After they saw Spencer Tracy in the play *The Last Mile*, Mrs Langham decided that the role of Killer Mears was custom-made for Gable. Reputedly, she arranged for him to take the part in the West Coast production of *The Last Mile*, and he was a sensation. As a result, Darryl F. Zanuck tested him for *Little Caesar* but complained about the shape of his ears, and did not sign him to a contract. Minna Wallis, however, did. She was not only a top agent but also the sister of the producer Hal Wallis. She got him the role of a nasty young villain in a Pathé Western, *The*

Painted Desert (1931), with William Boyd and Helen Twelvetrees. She then persuaded William Wellman to hire him for the part of a villainous chauffeur in Warner Brothers' *Night Nurse* (1931), in which he gave Barbara Stanwyck such a brutal beating that audiences were left gasping.

The release of *Night Nurse* was delayed for over a year, and by the time it came out Minna Wallis had got Gable a two-year contract, with options, at MGM. His first picture there was in a small role as Anita Page's husband, a hard-working laundryman in *The Easiest Way* (1931). His success in the part led him directly into *The Secret Six* (1931), in which he and John Mack Brown played reporters investigating underworld crime. The studio was pushing Brown because he had been a top athlete before entering films and had big movie star potential. Frances Marion, however, the scriptwriter of *The Secret Six* and the highest-paid person in her profession at that time, immediately saw Gable's galactic potential. Her husband, George Hill, was the film's director, and they quietly decided to give the stronger lines and better scenes to Gable rather than to Brown. The ruse worked. Gable's rough, tough, but sympathetic role was made to fit. Studio interest was diverted from Brown to Gable and the order went out to give him the big star build-up.

He fitted in well at MGM; his best friends there were the public relations man Howard

Far left: Gable as Rhett Butler in Gone With the Wind. *Left: with his third wife Carole Lombard. Above left: the rising star of 1931 in* A Free Soul *with Norma Shearer and Leslie Howard and* Possessed *(above) with Joan Crawford and Skeets Gallagher. Below: Fletcher Christian to Charles Laughton's Bligh in* Mutiny on the Bounty

Strickling and the director Victor Fleming, in whose company he frequently hunted and fished, golfed and sailed. The studio paid for the perfect set of dentures it was finally necessary for him to have; and also paid for surgery to pin back his ears.

Meanwhile Josephine Dillon had agreed to a divorce. She spoke of him with reluctant but calculated reticence:

'Clark told me frankly that he wished to marry Ria Langham because she could do more for him financially. He is hard to live with because his career and ambition always come first.'

Ria Langham became the second Mrs Clark Gable in New York on March 30, 1930, and they were married a second time in California on June 19, 1931, because of a legal hitch. Ria Langham queened it in Beverly Hills film society, which was fitting enough because by the end of 1931 her husband was the acknowledged King of Hollywood. He was a star who would be in the box-office top ten from 1932 to 1943, again from 1947 to 1949 after he

had returned from the war, and for one more year in 1955.

Most of the time MGM reserved Gable, drawing on his powerful masculine image, to co-star with their galaxy of female stars, and he developed powerful screen partnerships with three of their greatest stars. Joan Crawford and he were together in eight features, Myrna Loy was with him seven times, and Jean Harlow was with him six times.

Gable's off-screen relationships with Miss Loy and Miss Harlow were always platonic, friendly but strictly professional. Miss Crawford later confessed, however, that on several occasions when they were both free from personal obligations they nearly ran away and married, but on each occasion came to their senses in time – their careers mattered more.

Gable also starred with Lana Turner in four films, with Norma Shearer in three, with Rosalind Russell in three, Constance Bennett twice, and Helen Hayes twice. He made one appearance each with Greta Garbo and Jeanette MacDonald. He was, in fact, at some time or another teamed with every MGM female star except Marie Dressler.

Gable was at his best, however, in a man's world, leading the *Mutiny on the Bounty* (1935), sorting out the problems of the Air Force in *Command Decision* (1948), scouting Indian country in *Across the Wide Missouri* (1951). Also, say the name of Clark Gable and to most people it means Rhett Butler in *Gone With the Wind* (1939), or Peter Warne, the newspaper reporter he played in *It Happened One Night* (1934); yet he hadn't wanted to play them or *Bounty's* Fletcher Christian. These were the three pictures for which he was honoured with Oscar nominations (winning for *It Happened One Night*) – virtually the only three he fought against playing.

During the filming of *Gone With the Wind*, Gable was more excited when Ria divorced him for a settlement of $286,000. He was a free man before shooting was finished and drove with Carole Lombard to Kingman, Arizona, where they were quietly married on March, 29, 1939. They had known each other for nearly three years; it was no secret that they had been living together for most of that time, and were both still ecstatically happy. They bought a ranch in Encino and settled down; it seemed as if they would always be the perfect couple. World War II came, however, and Lombard threw herself into war work. She went out on the first War Bond tour after Pearl Harbor in 1942. Returning home, the plane crashed into a mountainside and everybody on it was killed.

Gable was half-crazy with grief. Lombard had teased him about getting involved in the war and now it was all he wanted to do. He took time off from the nearly completed *Somewhere I'll Find You* (1942) to get a firm hold of himself. Then he finished the picture, and eventually joined up in August 1942. He was assigned to Officers Candidate School in Miami, Florida, and went overseas with the Eighth Air Force in 1943. Seven months later he received the Distinguished Flying Cross and Air Medal for 'exceptionally meritorious achievement while participating in five separate bomber combat missions' over Germany. Gable was promoted to the rank of major and, discharged shortly afterwards, returned to work for MGM.

The studio did not know what to do with him: Gable had changed – so had the image of the movie hero. *Adventure* (1945), his comeback film co-starring him with Greer Garson, was a tedious, manufactured comedy. *The Hucksters* (1947), with Deborah Kerr and Ava Gardner, had its moments but was largely a bore. Next to *Parnell* (1937), *Homecoming* (1948) – his third post-war film – is probably his most tiresome and embarrassing picture. The next two were better: Gable seemed to be at ease in uniform with an all-male cast in *Command Decision* (1948); and in *Any Number Can Play* (1949), here as a casino owner. Most

Above left: Gable and Jean Harlow in Wife vs Secretary *(1936). Above: on the set of* Lone Star *(1952) with Ava Gardner. Above right: in* Across the Wide Missouri *(1951). Below, far left: with Spencer Tracy and Myrna Loy in* Test Pilot *(1938). Below left: with Barbara Stanwyck in* To Please a Lady *(1950). Below right: with (back row) Eli Wallach, Arthur Miller, John Huston, (front) Montgomery Clift, Marilyn Monroe, while making* The Misfits – *the last film for both Gable and Monroe*

of his later films were disappointing, however. Even *Mogambo* (1953), Ford's remake of *Red Dust* (1932), with Ava Gardner and Grace Kelly, which did very well at the box-office, was tame in comparison to the earlier version and had little 'bezazz' except Miss Gardner.

Gable was bitterly discontented during this period. He was also lonely, and committed a terrible and expensive error when, on December 21, 1949, he married a fourth time. The bride was Lady Sylvia Ashley, the widow of Douglas Fairbanks Sr. It is said that three weeks after the wedding Gable knew that he'd made a mistake. They were not divorced, however, until 1951 – an event which cost Gable a neat bundle. That same year Dore Schary replaced Louis B. Mayer as head of production at MGM. The stars began falling out of the MGM heavens and Gable's contract, expiring in 1954, was not renewed.

He became the most expensive freelance actor in the business, working for a percentage of the gross. His pictures, though largely ineffective, were better than any he had made at MGM after returning from the war, and they made money. Gable also fell in love, and married for the fifth time. His new wife was beautiful Kay Spreckels; there was much about her that was not unlike Carole Lombard and for the first time since Lombard's death Gable was really happy.

His last film, *The Misfits* (1961), written by Arthur Miller and directed by John Huston, was one of the best pictures he ever made. He played an ageing cowboy who is seeking one

Filmography
1923 Fighting Blood (series). '24 White Man; Forbidden Paradise. '25 Déclassée/The Social Exile; The Pacemakers (series); The Merry Widow; The Plastic Age; North Star. '31 The Painted Desert; Dance, Fools, Dance; The Easiest Way; The Finger Points; Laughing Sinners; The Secret Six; A Free Soul; Night Nurse; Sporting Blood; Susan Lenox: Her Fall and Rise (GB: The Rise of Helga); Possessed; Hell Divers. '32 Polly of the Circus; Strange Interlude (GB: Strange Interval); Red Dust; No Man of Her Own. '33 The White Sister; Hold Your Man; Night Flight; Dancing Lady. '34 Men in White; It Happened One Night; Manhattan Melodrama; Chained; Forsaking All Others. '35 After Office Hours; Call of the Wild; China Seas; Mutiny on the Bounty. '36 Wife vs Secretary/Wife versus Secretary; Screen Snapshots No. 10 (short); San Francisco; Cain and Mabel; Love on the Run. '37 Parnell; Saratoga. '38 Test Pilot; Too Hot to Handle. '39 Idiot's Delight; Gone With the Wind. '40 Strange Cargo; Boom Town; Comrade X. '41 They Met in Bombay; Honky Tonk. '42 Somewhere I'll Find You. '43 Combat America (military training short); Wings Up (propaganda short, incorporating footage from Combat America); Aerial Gunner (military training short). '45 Adventure. '47 The Hucksters. '48 Homecoming; Command Decision. '49 Any Number Can Play. '50 Key to the City; To Please a Lady. '51 Across the Wide Missouri; Callaway Went That-a-Way (guest) (GB: The Star Said No). '52 Lone Star. '53 Never Let Me Go (GB); Mogambo. '54 Betrayed. '55 Soldier of Fortune; The Tall Men. '56 The King and Four Queens. '57 Band of Angels. '58 Teacher's Pet; Run Silent, Run Deep. '59 But Not for Me. '60 It Started in Naples. '61 The Misfits.

last perfect moment on earth and finds it in a beautiful divorcee (Marilyn Monroe).

Gable had a good time making *The Misfits* but it was not an easy picture to work on. Filming it on location in Reno, the cast and crew had to put up with weather conditions of sheer hell – it was usually over 105°F. The action was far too strenuous for a man of Gable's years but he refused a double; Monroe, meanwhile, was exasperatingly difficult, never on time and unprofessional. But Gable was content. His wife was pregnant, and he went around announcing, 'It's going to be a boy'.

It was a boy – named John Clark Gable – but his father never lived to see him. Two days after completing his part in *The Misfits*, Clark Gable suffered a massive heart attack and died on November 16, 1960, aged 59.

Between 1957 and 1961 many of the screen heart-throbs of the Thirties and Forties died, including Ronald Colman, Gary Cooper, Tyrone Power, Errol Flynn and Humphrey Bogart. But it was Gable's death that really signified the end of that generation of all-male, all-action movie heroes – for Gable alone had been the King of Hollywood.

DeWITT BODEEN

The Steve McQueen Affair

'Speed is incredible and beautiful. Slip-streaming around a turn in the middle of a pack is what separates the men from the boys. If you can't cut in you may have to back out. It's as simple as that.' The words of Steve McQueen, talking about his love for race-driving and perhaps about his career as a film actor, are the words of the most realistic of superstars. Tough, laconic, and independent, McQueen always seemed likely to win the race . . .

The career of Steve McQueen seems a classic example of the American Dream made real, of a small-town boy triumphing over adversity – broken home, poor education – to become one of the richest and most sought-after superstars in the world. He was a man who finally found the love he never knew as a child in the adoration of the millions of fans who flocked to almost every action-packed screen adventure graced by his rugged, tanned but quizzical good looks. His shocking early death at 50 from cancer robbed the cinema of an exceptional personality who had been steadily maturing into an actor of a wider range and sensitivity

than his scripts demanded, and one keenly interested in all aspects of the productions in which he starred.

The Indianapolis kid

Terence Stephen McQueen was born into a farming family in Indianapolis on March 24, 1930; his father left before the baby was six months old and never saw his son again. His mother was only 19 and went to work in California, entrusting her child to his great-uncle, who raised him on his farm and saw that he had a basic education in the local one-room school. When he was nine, he was taken

back to Indianapolis by his mother, a move that seems to have propelled him into delinquency. He joined small gangs, took to petty thieving and the kinds of minor hooliganism shown in Fellini's *I Vitelloni* (1953, *The Spivs*) – a film McQueen admired for its accurate depiction of teenagers hanging around on street corners whistling at girls. His mother remarried and took Steve to Los Angeles, but he had become an unruly, rebellious youth and had to be sent to a reform school at Chino where he spent two years – when he was not playing truant. The school's tough regime made a valuable impression, however, and in later years McQueen often revisited it to talk to the boys and present awards he had endowed, also regularly keeping in touch with former inmates and helping them when in trouble.

After a brief unsuccessful reunion with his mother, McQueen ran away to sea on a tanker, and took several odd jobs before enlisting in the Marine Corps at 17; he worked as a tank-driver and mechanic, which prompted a life-long interest in vehicles, especially motorcycles and racing. In 1950 he went to live in the bohemian Greenwich Village district of New York where, between low-paid casual jobs as a bartender and TV repair-man, he was first introduced to acting by a girlfriend. Through her he met Sanford Meisner, director of the Neighbourhood Playhouse drama-school, who enrolled him after an audition, immediately recognizing his tough and yet strangely child-like qualities. Meisner found McQueen his first professional part, a one-line role in a Yiddish play on Second Avenue which paid $40 a week. He subsequently won a scholarship to the Uta Hagen-Herbert Berghof Dramatic School in Manhattan, and two years later was selected as one of five out of five thousand applicants to the Actors' Studio, the famous 'Method' workshop run by Lee Strasberg. About this time a diving accident impaired his hearing but he overcame this hardship and embarked on a modestly successful theatrical career, acting in summer stock, appearing in several television dramas and eventually making it to Broadway in 1956 – replacing Ben Gazzara as the young drug-addict in *A Hatful of Rain*.

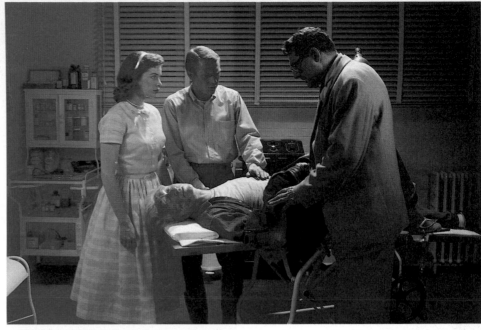

A wanted man

After his marriage to actress and singer Neile Adams, McQueen moved to Hollywood and won his first film role as a $19-a-day extra in Robert Wise's *Somebody Up There Likes Me* (1956), the life-story of boxer Rocky Graziano. In 1958, billed as Steven McQueen, he played the lead part of a Jewish law student – with John Barrymore's son Drew cast as his Catholic, criminal friend – in a confused Harold Robbins melodrama, *Never Love a Stranger*. He received better notices in an independently produced, low-budget thriller, *The Great St Louis Bank Robbery* (1959), and had turned in the most natural performance in a near-classic science-fiction B movie, *The Blob* (1958), combatting a carnivorous jelly from Outer Space

Left: Hilts 'the Cooler King' finally comes to grief in The Great Escape. *Above right: an early part for McQueen in* The Blob. *Right: publicity shot for* The Cincinnati Kid *with Ann-Margret and Tuesday Weld. Below: with Faye Dunaway in* The Thomas Crown Affair

and some equally ludicrous dialogue.

McQueen's break into stardom came, in fact, not in the cinema but on television, thanks to his creation in 1957 of the role of bounty-hunter Josh Randall in the CBS Western series *Wanted – Dead or Alive*. McQueen managed to make the character sympathetic – a man doing his job, however sordid, as best he could. It was a part he was to repeat, with variations, in several of his films. The director John Sturges saw McQueen in *Wanted – Dead or Alive* and subsequently gave him the scene-stealing part of a cheeky, scrounging soldier (originally meant for Sammy Davis Jr) in his war film *Never So Few* (1959). The production was designed as the Hollywood launch for Gina Lollobrigida and also starred Frank Sinatra and Peter Lawford, but it was McQueen who caught the eye with the deft timing of a practised comedian – a very different characterization from the moody men of action he was usually to portray.

Sturges probably did most to further McQueen's film career. He brilliantly cast him as one of *The Magnificent Seven* (1960), his outstandingly successful Western remake of Kurosawa's *Shichinin No Samurai* (1954, *Seven Samurai*). McQueen immediately caught the public's imagination as a deadly gunfighter, cool and calculating but with sufficient wry touches to offset the playing of the film's established star Yul Brynner. He was quickly hailed as the successor to James Dean, and his offscreen behaviour – his rebelliousness, independence and idiosyncrasies in speech and dress – helped project a hell-raising image.

Into top gear

After *Never So Few*, McQueen's only other out-and-out comic role was as another larcenous but lovable man in uniform, a peacetime navy lieutenant in *The Honeymoon Machine* (1961) who uses his warship's computer to break the roulette bank at Venice and nearly provokes a Russian attack in the process. But he seemed more at ease in straight war dramas – such as Don Siegel's *Hell Is for Heroes* (1962) – and confirmed his impact with critics and millions of moviegoers with his daredevil motorcycle stunts in *The Great Escape* (1963), in which

Sturges co-starred him with James Garner and Richard Attenborough as one of the Allied prisoners-of-war tunnelling to freedom from Stalag Luft North. As 'the Cooler King' (who constantly tries to break out alone and is thrown into the 'cooler' when recaptured), McQueen had a part completely in character – and himself suggested the famous chase sequence when he makes his getaway, though, as in his later pictures, he actually performed less of the exploits than meet the eye, reluctantly accepting a double for the most dangerous takes. He still won the Best Actor award at the Moscow Film Festival, however.

In his next couple of films McQueen strengthened his appeal to female audiences with romantic roles for the director Robert Mulligan – partnering Natalie Wood in *Love With the Proper Stranger* (1963), where he played a footloose musician reluctant to marry his pregnant girlfriend, and appearing as the violent hillbilly with Lee Remick as his wife in *Baby, the Rain Must Fall* (1965), an offbeat drama unsure of its convictions. McQueen had by this time earned enough to invest in several small businesses and start his own production companies to buy or develop film projects. But he took a year's holiday with his family before beginning his next film, Norman Jewison's suspensful *The Cincinnati Kid* (1965), the story of a young stud-poker player pitted against a champion card-sharp played by Edward G. Robinson, whose very presence managed to upstage even McQueen's delicately judged performance.

In 1966 he worked again with director Robert Wise in *The Sand Pebbles*, this time a costly and elaborate reconstruction of an incident involving an American gunboat blockaded on the Yangtze River during the Chinese Civil War in 1926. Although the cumbersome production went down like the Titanic in cinemas all over the world, McQueen clearly

Below: the climax of Nevada Smith *with McQueen – a young version of the character played by Alan Ladd in* The Carpetbaggers *(1964) – about to take his revenge on the men who murdered his father and Indian mother. Right: as the ex-convict who, unreformed, gets together with his wife (Ali McGraw) and robs a bank in Sam Peckinpah's violent crime thriller* The Getaway

revelled in his well-observed role as the gunboat's chief mechanic. 'He dominates every foot of the film on which his image is imprinted', the director commented, and the star was subsequently nominated for an Academy Award for his magnetic portrayal of the decent but doomed sailor.

Crowning moments
This stage of his career saw McQueen able to choose his own roles and, with the backing of his own company Solar, ensure that any picture would adequately showcase his talents. For Henry Hathaway and Solar he played the title-role in *Nevada Smith* (1966) a latter-day revenge Western inspired by a character in Harold Robbins' novel *The Carpetbaggers*; his rifle-toting, Christ-like pose for the film's publicity became a popular icon. Solar also co-produced *The Thomas Crown Affair* (1968), a well-liked thriller flashily directed by Norman Jewison, which gave McQueen some memorably erotic scenes with Faye Dunaway, cast as the insurance investigator using all her charms to counter his suave and sexy crooked businessman. 'He's the most difficult actor I ever worked with' Jewison later remarked.

Racing remained a ruling passion of McQueen's life, despite the fears of his wife and the studios' insurance agents, and it was one he persisted in pursuing on the screen – with unforgettable results in *Bullitt* (1968), which might have been an ordinary police thriller but for its amazing car chase up and down the steep streets of San Francisco, but with a notable lack of success in *Le Mans* (1971). This is a dull, near-documentary re-creation of the 24-hour French race that had become an obsessive goal for McQueen but proved less engrossing for his public. Its box-office failure contributed to a spell of self-doubt for the actor, who found the demands of stardom an increasing burden. But working twice in 1972 for Sam Peckinpah, a kindred unruly spirit, brought him a different, more mature type of role – as the declining rodeo rider in *Junior Bonner* – and a new wife (Neile had left him in 1970) in Ali McGraw, co-star of *The Getaway*, a violent and amoral robbery-and-chase movie.

Around this time McQueen joined with Barbra Streisand, Sidney Poitier and Paul Newman in their First Artists Production (FAP) company and remained one of the world's most highly paid performers throughout the Seventies, though his films became less frequent. He took the title role in *Papillon* (1973), the blockbuster adaptation of a real-life escape from Devil's Island, and played the fire-chief hero of *The Towering Inferno* (1974), the disaster movie that proved far from disastrous at the world's box-offices. But McQueen was not at all satisfied with the way his career was going and tried to strike out into more intellectual movies.

Million dollar McQueen

Living as a virtual recluse, he turned down many pictures after *The Towering Inferno* and even refused the lead in *Apocalypse Now* (1979) by demanding $3 million for three weeks work, an unheard-of sum in 1976 when production began (though he earned more than that on *The Hunter* (1980).

He returned to the screen after an absence of nearly four years in a modest and valiant version of Ibsen's play *An Enemy of the People* (1977), in which he was a heavily bearded and almost unrecognizable as the doctor fighting hypocrisy in a small Norwegian spa. Poorly released and critically undervalued, it was nevertheless a fine, impressive enterprise and suggested new avenues for McQueen to explore. Indeed, he planned to film Harold

Below: McQueen as a tired and grizzled bounty-hunter in Tom Horn. Bottom, from left to right: as a brooding American racing driver in his pet project Le Mans, a virtually plotless, semi-documentary re-creation of the big race; as Papillon, the prisoner who escapes from a nightmare existence on Devil's Island; in his final film The Hunter as the man who tracks down crooks who jump bail

Pinter's play *Old Times*, but a bitter lawsuit with FAP obliged him to make *Tom Horn* (1979), another Western about a bounty-hunter, instead.

The hunter and the hunted

He was already ill during the making of *The Hunter*; this final film, though not especially distinguished, shows a tender, rueful quality amid the knockabout heroics and McQueen's instinctive feel for comedy gives an appealing edge to the true story of a modern bounty-hunter and his crazy capers.

After the rare lung disease mesothelioma was diagnosed late in 1979, the actor characteristically tried to fight off the cancer for a year, undergoing strenuous exercise, diet and medication in a controversial treatment which at first seemed to work. He died of a heart attack after a stomach operation, on November 7, 1980, in a Mexican hospital, with his third wife model Barbara Minty and his two eldest children at his side.

It was a tragic end for a star whose life had celebrated manly virtues and whose youthful high-spirits and deep-rooted insecurity had matured into courage and determination, both on the screen and off. His death was the sadder in view of his frustrated efforts to use his star status to better effect. At the height of his fame he had no illusions about his role as a star and was never convinced that acting was a thing for a grown man to be doing.

PHILLIP BERGSON

Filmography
1956 Somebody Up There Likes Me (uncredited). '58 Never Love a Stranger; The Blob. '59 The Great St Louis Bank Robbery; Never So Few. '60 The Magnificent Seven. '61 The Honeymoon Machine. '62 Hell Is for Heroes; The War Lover (GB). '63 The Great Escape; A Soldier in the Rain; Love With the Proper Stranger. '65 Baby, the Rain Must Fall; The Cincinnati Kid. '66 Nevada Smith; The Sand Pebbles. '68 The Thomas Crown Affair; Bullitt. '69 The Reivers. '71 On Any Sunday (doc); Le Mans. '72 Junior Bonner; The Getaway. '73 Papillon. '74 The Towering Inferno. '77 An Enemy of the People (+exec. prod). '79 Tom Horn (+exec. prod). '80 The Hunter.

Born in 1925 in Cleveland, Ohio, Newman studied acting at the Yale University Drama School and at Lee Strasberg's Actors' Studio. After appearing in many live television dramas and on Broadway, he made his screen debut in *The Silver Chalice* (1955). After his second film, *Somebody Up There Likes Me* (1956), his stardom was assured, but Newman's major decade was really the Sixties when he created his four most memorable characters in *The Hustler* (1961), *Hud* (1963), *Cool Hand Luke* (1967) and *Butch Cassidy and the Sundance Kid* (1969), at the same time solidifying his clearly recognizable image.

This image was one of moody rebelliousness, rugged individualism, cool detachment and, above all, overpowering sex-appeal. Newman filled the vacuum created by the death of James Dean and decline of Marlon Brando. He ascended over others because he was best able to embody the alienation and restlessness of his era while possessing a traditional beauty that most of his contemporaries lacked. Paul Newman was simultaneously the perfect modern anti-hero and the link with a glamorous Hollywood that was rapidly fading into memory.

Dr Jekyll . . .

His screen persona and private personality have often been opposites. Like other Actors' Studio alumni, he considers himself a 'cerebral' actor and regards each role as an agonizing 'study session', yet he has played many spontaneous, uninhibited characters. He has also often portrayed supremely confident and charming types even though he is privately rather shy and insecure. Committed passionately to liberal and humanitarian causes, Newman has created a substantial gallery of men who are committed mainly to themselves, and although he has been married to one woman – actress Joanne Woodward – since 1958, his characters attack, insult and discard women, subordinating them entirely to male ambition.

Ambition is in fact a key aspect of the Newman image. Some of his characters are born on the wrong side of the tracks and pursue the American Dream of wealth and status, as in *The Young Philadelphians* (1959) and *Sweet Bird of Youth* (1962). Others are not necessarily interested in money – the goal may be winning a pool match in *The Hustler* or a motor race in *Winning* (1969), executing a mission such as helping Jewish refugees to enter Palestine in *Exodus* (1960), or excelling at music, the aim of Ram Bowen (Newman) in *Paris Blues* (1961) – but the means are similar. These men set aside considerations of love, family, humanity and morality, and push forward ruthlessly, alienating themselves from society in the process.

However, Newman's performances inspire identification with even his most arrogant and selfish characters' problems and obsessions. Many of his 'nasty' men at least have the

Right: Big Daddy (Burl Ives) learns he has cancer when his angry son (Newman) tells him during a confrontation in Cat on a Hot Tin Roof. *Centre right: ageing playboy Chance Wayne (Newman) and his lover (Shirley Knight) in* Sweet Bird of Youth. *Far right: private eye* Harper *closes in on his quarry aided by Fay Estabrook (Shelley Winters)*

Paul Newman

First, the eyes; dazzlingly bright blue and seeming – as one columnist put it – 'as if they have just finished taking a shower'. Then, the classic profile and sensual mouth, suggesting nothing less than a Greek statue or perhaps even Michelangelo's David. At the start, Paul Newman's success derived largely from his extraordinary looks and it took audiences – and critics – some time to discover the serious actor behind the façade

saving characteristic of recognizing their nastiness and turning it into charm; Newman's boyishness and sense of humour make them engaging. Of course this involvement is generated partly by his looks: he may characterize obnoxious, irresponsible, rough types, but his features usually suggest intelligence and sensitivity.

In addition, his portrayals of Brick in *Cat on a*

Left: the famous features that have helped ensure Newman's continuing success. Below: in The Sting *he played an ingenious con-man out to trick a big-time gangster. Below right: as a pool shark in* The Hustler, *Newman scored one of his biggest hits*

Hot Tin Roof, Billy the Kid in *The Left-Handed Gun* (both 1958) and Luke in *Cool Hand Luke* evoke sympathy because of the extreme loneliness that their actions bring them. A remarkable number of his characters are also humanized by having to undergo severe physical punishment: he has his thumbs broken in *The Hustler*; his face smashed in *Sweet Bird of Youth*; is dragged by a horse in *The Life and Times of Judge Roy Bean* (1972); and is continually and mercilessly tortured in *Cool Hand Luke*. The extreme degradation and pain creates an atmosphere of vulnerability that facilitates audience identification.

Perhaps the most important reason for the appeal of Newman's heroes and anti-heroes is

that they seem to have embodied the general moods of their times. In key Fifties roles, playing characters like Rocky Graziano (*Somebody Up There Likes Me*) and Billy the Kid, he slipped into the Brando/Dean mould – the confused, inarticulate rebel who strikes out at the world without knowing why. Rocky's alienation from his uncaring father and Billy's general difficulty with father-figures struck another responsive chord at the time, allying them with Dean's characters as well as with other troubled youths in Fifties cinema.

Rebel with a cause
In the Sixties, Newman's image evolved into that of the relatively *intelligent* rebel, more in

Profile of a winner

control of himself and better able to define his cause. 'Fast' Eddie (*The Hustler*), Chance Wayne (*Sweet Bird of Youth*) and Hud Bannon (*Hud*) *can* describe what motivates them and although they are hardly set on improving society their very ability to articulate may have made them connect with youth during the Kennedy era.

Ironically, Newman's stated intentions in playing these ruthless opportunists was to have the audience condemn them. He hoped to show that men who have everything impressive to fellow Americans – attractiveness, charm, virility, an ability to seduce women and to feel equally comfortable drinking with the guys – often have 'the seed of corruption' in them, and succeed only at the cost of their souls. Yet they were vibrant, magnetic, and audiences were drawn to them.

The quintessence was Hud, the amoral modern Texan who could have been a prototype for J.R. Ewing (Larry Hagman) of the popular television series *Dallas*; arrogant, opportunistic, Machiavellian, incapable of warmth or affection, rotten to the core – and yet completely captivating. Newman pulled out all the stops, bringing to perfection his familiar characteristics: the cynical, aloof manner; the nasty, contemptuous voice; the sly, insinuating smil ; the icy stare; the insolent sexiness. The ads proclaimed, 'Paul Newman *is* Hud'. Their assumption may have been inaccurate, but for audiences Newman a d Hud were one.

'Cool' in the coolers

In the later Sixties, perhaps as a reflection of society's growing cynicism, most of Newman's films abandoned even the attempt to condemn their amoral protagonists. Harper, the slightly

Above: Newman as Luke Jackson in Cool Hand Luke, *the story of a convict's two years hard labour on a chain gang and his eventual death. Below: in* Hud *he plays an amoral rancher whose debauched way of life finally drives his young nephew (Brandon de Wilde) away from the ranch*

Above: Newman with Joanne Woodward on the set of Rachel, Rachel, *in which she plays a repressed schoolmistress. Below:* The Life and Times of Judge Roy Bean *starred Newman as the Judge and Roddy McDowell as Frank Gass but the beer-drinking bear stole the limelight*

Right: Newman and Woodward shooting a scene for WUSA *as they 'speed' along, the back-projected scenery lending it authenticity. Below right: in an effort to escape his image, he played a foul-mouthed hockey-coach keeping a fading team together in* Slap Shot

worn, sardonic private eye in the 1966 movie of the same name, was a perfect embodiment of Sixties 'cool': anti-heroic and brutally exploitative, he is the master of flippancy, nastiness and the new art of the 'put on'. Now audiences were meant to regard the character as the hero, and they did, making Harper one of Newman's most popular roles.

Moviegoers also responded enthusiastically to *Cool Hand Luke*. Anti-establishment and anti-authority, Luke breaks the law not because of social deprivation – the excuse in most Thirties' films – but because it gives him something to do. The act of rebellion has become its own justification, making Luke an appropriate anti-hero for the late Sixties. Here Newman had returned to the silent rebel type, but unlike the Fifties rebel Luke chose to remain silent. He is neither confused nor directionless but is an intelligent individual

who elects to separate himself from the rest of humanity. Yet, as opposed to 'Fast' Eddie and Hud, he has no definite goal and unintentionally becomes a martyr.

Coping with comedy
As Luke, Newman gave his most relaxed performance so far, but in *Butch Cassidy and the Sundance Kid* he is even looser and more casual. Butch, a ludicrous, failed opportunist and hopeless romantic, is a fascinating comic version of Newman's ambitious dreamers. In previous attempts at comedy – such as *Rally 'Round the Flag, Boys!* (1958) and *A New Kind of Love* (1963) – Newman was stiff and forced, but here he is spontaneous and appealing. This derives partly from the fact that Butch is an easy-going, naturally funny fellow instead of an exaggerated comic character, and partly from the pairing with Robert Redford, which

creates an immensely attractive camaraderie that is rare in Newman's career. A huge success, the film had everything for contemporary audiences; hip cleverness, a casual attitude towards crime and violence, blundering anti-heroes instead of the traditional genre types, and good-natured but appropriately distanced relationships.

In the Seventies, Newman remained on the list of top box-office stars and two of his films, *The Sting* (1973) and *The Towering Inferno* (1974), far surpassed the grosses of *Butch Cassidy and the Sundance Kid*. Still, *The Sting*'s success may have been due more to the Newman/Redford partnership, or even to Redford's popularity alone, than to Newman's appeal, and *The Towering Inferno* did not seem to depend on the drawing power of its stars – the appeal of the disaster-movie being well established by then. Otherwise, Newman's only big hit since 1969 has been *Slap Shot* (1977), in which his late-career relaxation and sense of fun were strong contributions to his characterization of a hockey-coach.

His other Seventies work includes *The Drowning Pool* (1975) – a sequel to *Harper* that failed to recapture the original's magic – and several films in which Newman played such extremely unpleasant characters that audiences could not identify with them: a cynical, corrupt and thoroughly vicious opportunist in *WUSA* (1970); a stubborn reactionary in *Sometimes a Great Notion* (1971); and an exceedingly sadistic, violent man in *The Mackintosh Man* (1973).

His most challenging film in recent years has been *Buffalo Bill and the Indians . . . or Sitting Bull's History Lesson* (1976), a cynical exploration of show business in which Newman, adopting an ironic stance towards his character, seems to be exploring his own identity as a superstar. However, the film was so unremittingly bitter that it failed to find an audience.

New directions
During the late Sixties Newman decided to try his hand in another area and he has achieved some critical success as a director. *Rachel, Rachel* (1968) and *The Effect of Gamma Rays on Man-in-the-Moon Marigolds* (1972) are gentle, richly emotional and melancholy – yet never depressing – slices of ordinary people's lives. Both indicate a mature visual sensibility and feature excellent performances by Joanne Woodward who also appeared in the fourth film Newman directed, a television feature entitled *The Shadow Box* (1980). *Sometimes a Great Notion*, the story of the problems faced by a logging family, combined precise character portraits and vigorous outdoor adventure in the Howard Hawks mode.

The remainder of his acting career will be interesting to follow. In his mid-fifties he has retained his looks and physique and, like many traditional male stars, is enduring as a leading man well into his later years; his romances with women quite a few years his junior in *The Mackintosh Man* and *When Time Ran Out . . .* (1980) are surely in the Gable Cooper/Grant tradition. On the other hand, he has always wanted to be a character actor and since this will undoubtedly be forced upon him by age, he may enjoy the opportunity. Judge Roy Bean, a combination of leading man – attractive, gentle, charming a young woman – and character personality – grizzled, gruff, befriending a bear – is a suitable point of departure.

MICHAEL KERBEL

Filmography
1955 The Silver Chalice. **'56** Somebody Up There Likes Me; The Rack. **'57** The Helen Morgan Story (GB: Both Ends of the Candle); Until They Sail. **'58** The Long Hot Summer; The Left-Handed Gun; Cat on a Hot Tin Roof; Rally 'Round the Flag, Boys! **'59** The Young Philadelphians (GB: The City Jungle). **'60** From the Terrace; Exodus. **'61** The Hustler; Paris Blues. **'62** Sweet Bird of Youth; Hemingway's Adventures of a Young Man/Adventures of a Young Man. **'63** Hud; A New Kind of Love; The Prize. **'64** What a Way to Go!; The Outrage. **'65** Lady L (USA-FR-IT). **'66** Harper (GB: The Moving Target); Torn Curtain. **'67** Hombre; Cool Hand Luke. **'68** The Secret War of Harry Frigg; Rachel, Rachel (dir; +prod. only). **'69** Winning (+co-exec. prod); Butch Cassidy and the Sundance Kid (+co-exec. prod). **'70** King . . . a Filmed Record: Montgomery to Memphis/Martin Luther King (doc) (co-narr. only); WUSA (+co-prod). **'71** They Might Be Giants (co-prod. only); Sometimes a Great Notion (+dir; +co-exec. prod) (GB: Never Give an Inch). **'72** Pocket Money (+co-exec. prod); The Effect of Gamma Rays on Man-in-the-Moon Marigolds (dir; +prod. only); The Life and Times of Judge Roy Bean (+co-exec. prod). **'73** The Mackintosh Man (GB); The Sting. **'74** The Towering Inferno. **'75** The Drowning Pool (+co-exec. prod). **'76** Silent Movie (guest); Buffalo Bill and the Indians . . . or Sitting Bull's History Lesson. **'77** Slap Shot. **'79** Quintet. **'80** When Time Ran Out . . .; Fort Apache, the Bronx.

Olivier's Heights

Left: Olivier, sporting a medieval haircut, studies the script of Henry V, *which he directed and starred in. Above: Henry at the siege of Harfleur*

Laurence Olivier's towering achievements in the theatre have overshadowed his work in the cinema. Yet whether in his own daring adaptations from Shakespeare, or in his many superbly realized romantic and character roles, Olivier has time and again proved his great talents on film

Spencer Tracy once called Olivier 'the greatest screen actor of them all', a tribute that is particularly remarkable in that it comes from the one actor who could legitimately lay claim to the title. Yet because Olivier has always considered himself first and foremost a stage actor (a consideration for which he was rewarded with the first peerage ever given to an actor), critics have been inclined to regard his screen career as of secondary importance.

It comes, therefore, as something of a surprise to realize that Olivier has thus far made nearly sixty films. The list is dominated by his three major Shakespeare adaptations – *Henry V* (1944), *Hamlet* (1948) and *Richard III* (1956) – but his screen work began as far back as 1930, in which year he played in a 'quota quickie' called *Too Many Crooks*.

His career can be divided into four phases. First, in the Thirties, came his films as a romantic juvenile lead: there are roughly fifteen of these, leading up to William Wyler's *Wuthering Heights* (1939) which was the first production to give Olivier any real respect for the cinema. Until then it had been on his own admission a place to make money in between the stage appearances that were his *raison d'être* as an actor. After some early and best-forgotten comedies, such as *The Temporary Widow* (1930) and *Potiphar's Wife* (1931), he had been ignominiously sacked by Greta Garbo from *Queen Christina* in 1933, thereby confirming his own belief that he was not cut out to be a film star.

Despite one early attempt at screen Shakespeare (as Orlando in Paul Czinner's *As You Like It*, 1936, opposite the enchantingly miscast Elisabeth Bergner) the Thirties were not a very happy time for Olivier; although his prestige as a stage actor continued to grow, he was generally only ever considered for film roles that Leslie Howard or Ronald Colman were unwilling or unable to accept. Not until the meeting with Wyler did he find a director who could teach him the basic techniques of film acting. Until then, 'stagey' is the word that best describes much of his screen work, even in such acknowledged successes as *Fire Over England* (1937), the first of the three films he made with his future second wife Vivien Leigh.

But then came Wyler and *Wuthering Heights*, though again Olivier only got to play Heathcliff after Ronald Colman proved unavailable and Robert Newton had done a poor test for the role. Olivier's acting won him the first of nine Oscar nominations.

'Looking back', he said later, 'I was snobbish about films until *Wuthering Heights* . . . then, gradually, I came to see that film was a different medium and that if one treated it as such and tried to learn it humbly, with an open mind, one could work in it. I saw that it could use the best that was going; it was Wyler who gave me the simple thought – "if you do it right, you can do anything". And if he hadn't said that I'd never have done *Henry V* five years later.'

In the meantime came *Rebecca*, *Pride and Prejudice* (both 1940) and *That Hamilton Woman!* (1941) as well as one or two guest appearances for the war effort in Britain. There is little doubt that had Olivier stayed in Hollywood he could have become another of the screen's great romantic Englishmen. But, as he was once quoted as saying, somewhat uncharitably. 'I don't wish to become just another film star like dear Cary'; if he were going to act in front of a camera again, it would be on his own terms and those terms were now Shakespearean.

Rooted in an English classical tradition (Olivier was born, the son of a clergyman, in Dorking on May 22, 1907) he began to look upon the filming – and therefore the popularizing – of Shakespeare as something of a personal crusade. He initially hoped to involve Vivien Leigh (whom he had married in the USA in 1940 after divorcing his first wife, the

and to cast the celebrated music-hall comedian George Robey as Falstaff was an indication of considerable courage in a producer-director making his first film.

Though the print cost of *Henry V* was not to be recovered for several years, its critical success encouraged Olivier to make *Hamlet*. He had doubts about his suitability for the lead, commenting that his style of acting was 'more suited to stronger character roles rather than the lyrical, poetic Hamlet'. These feelings were echoed by some critics, although James Agee thought that 'a man who can do what Olivier does for Shakespeare (and for those who treasure or will yet learn to treasure Shakespeare) is certainly among the more valuable men of his time'. The film won a total of four Oscars.

Richard III, the last of Olivier's major Shakespeare films, and his own personal favourite, was made in 1956 for Alexander Korda. This had been one of Olivier's greatest stage successes, but he again only took on the direction

Above: Olivier with Mina Burnett in his first film, Too Many Crooks. *Right: Greer Garson, Olivier and Frieda Inescort in* Pride and Prejudice, *made at the height of his Hollywood success. Below: Olivier's every word and gesture bespoke malevolence in his portrayal of* Richard III

actress Jill Esmond) in his plans. Their acting partnership had established them both at the head of their profession, though there was always to be some doubt about her strength in his company on stage. On the screen, however, they were sadly never to work together again after *That Hamilton Woman!*; Leigh's triumph as Scarlett O'Hara in *Gone With the Wind* (1939) led the owner of her contract, David O. Selznick, to refuse to allow her to appear in 'insignificant' roles. When compared to Scarlett, even Ophelia was deemed 'insignificant'.

For this reason Olivier was unable to cast Leigh as Princess Katherine in his first attempt

after a more experienced man (in this case Carol Reed) had declined the challenge. The film opened to considerable critical acclaim on both sides of the Atlantic. In the USA, following an unprecedented deal with American TV, the film was first shown by NBC, who interrupted it for three General Motors ads, one for a car battery 'more powerful than all the horses in *King Richard*'.

Sadly, however, none of the Shakespeare films had done well enough at the box-office to encourage production companies to provide Olivier with the money to make an adaptation of *Macbeth*.

The two final periods of his film-making career can best be divided into the films in which he played sizeable parts and those in which he guest-starred. In the former group are nineteen post-war films, of which only five were original, modern-dress screenplays: Peter Glenville's *Term of Trial* (1962), Otto Preminger's *Bunny Lake Is Missing* (1965), Joseph Mankiewicz's *Sleuth* (1973), John Schlesinger's *Marathon Man* (1976) and Franklin Schaffner's *The Boys From Brazil* (1978). This statistic may help to explain why Olivier is still thought of in primarily stage terms though many years have elapsed since his last theatrical appearance.

Carrie (1952) reunited Olivier with Wyler,

to film Shakespeare, *Henry V*. In addition he was unable to obtain the services of Wyler as director; this setback led him to take on the mantle of director as well as the lead role. Indeed, as film historian Roger Manvell has noted, the film might never have been made at all had it not been for a volatile Italian lawyer called Filippo del Giudice, who had earlier persuaded Noel Coward to make *In Which We Serve* (1942) and was now looking for another patriotic classic to coincide with the D-Day

landings in Normandy.

Working to a budget of £300,000 (which was only exceeded by one-third) Olivier cut Shakespeare's text by about one-quarter, adding to it only a spectacular Agincourt battle sequence (shot in Ireland) and the death of Falstaff, which he lifted from the end of *Henry IV Part II* to serve as a kind of soundtrack-flashback to explain the old man's disgrace. The decision to start and end the film within the confines of Shakespeare's Globe Theatre,

who had originally wanted 'dear Cary' for the role. Nonetheless, Olivier's performance, as a man inadvertently destroyed by the woman he loves, indicated the kind of screen actor Olivier could still be if he chose to put his mind to it. Of his subsequent features *The Entertainer*, which he made for Tony Richardson in 1960, represents Olivier at his absolute non-Shakespearian best. The part of Archie Rice, a down-at-heel pier comic, was one that he had first created on stage three years earlier. At that time the notion of Britain's leading classical actor allying himself with the playwright John Osborne, a well-known 'angry young man', caused considerable press disquiet. However Olivier had recognized that in *The Entertainer* Osborne had created one of the great roles of all time:

'You see this face? It can split open with warmth and humanity. It can sing, and tell the worst, unfunniest stories in the world to a

great mob of dead, drab erks and it doesn't matter, it doesn't matter because – look at my eyes. I'm dead behind these eyes, dead, just like the whole inert shoddy lot out there.'

Olivier's performance in this film remains convincing proof of his greatness on camera. Since this film, Olivier has appeared in *Term of Trial* (1962), a kind of latterday *Carrie*, and starred in some film versions of famous National Theatre productions, such as *Othello* (1965), *The Dance of Death* (1969) and *Three Sisters* (1970) – all of which hovered, in Dilys Powell's phrase, 'on the very margin of cinema'. He then made a return to major screen roles as a player of macabre practical

Above left: Olivier and his second wife Vivien Leigh. Top left: Jean Simmons and Olivier in Spartacus. *Top: the part of Archie Rice in* The Entertainer *provided Olivier with one of his finest roles. Above: Olivier directs a scene from* Three Sisters *featuring his third wife, Joan Plowright*

jokes in *Sleuth*, the two-handed thriller with Michael Caine (who said that acting with him was like acting with God), a sadistic Nazi dentist in *Marathon Man*, and an Austrian Jew on the track of a Nazi war criminal in *The Boys From Brazil*.

On the guest-starring front his performance

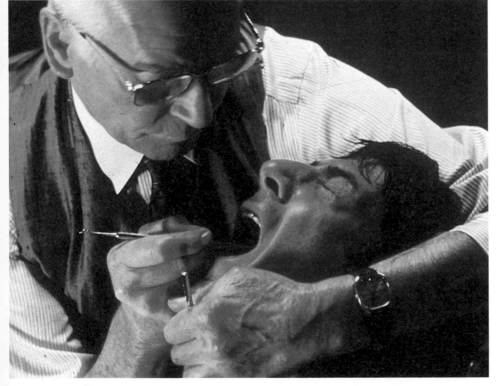

Below left: A student (Dustin Hoffman) falls victim to the tender mercies of Olivier's Nazi dentist in Marathon Man. *Left: Michael Caine and Olivier confront each other in a scene from* Sleuth. *Above: Olivier, playing a Dutch doctor, tends British paratroopers wounded at Arnhem in* A Bridge Too Far

birthdays might have talked of the pleasures of returning home, but not Olivier. How many other actors could have gone from Shakespeare to Harold Robbins on screen and survived the descent in reasonably good shape?

'Between good and great acting is fixed an inexorable gulf which may be crossed only by the select, whose visas are in order: Olivier pole-vaults across it in a single hair-raising animal leap', wrote Kenneth Tynan, while another critic has commented:

'Olivier looks like a man who could lynch a crowd; he resembles a panther – just when you know where he is and that you've got him cornered, he springs out at you from some totally different direction.'

And that, in essence, is also the story of his screen career.　　　　SHERIDAN MORLEY

---

as the Mahdi in *Khartoum* (1966) was perhaps a deliberate reminder of his then-current stage Othello, also very gutteral and way over the top, and here as in *Spartacus* (1960), in which he plays a homosexual Roman general, it seems fair to assume that for Olivier, epic acting means overacting. His other guest-starring work has been only occasionally distinguished (Richard Attenborough got a remarkable performance out of him as the old Dutch doctor in *A Bridge Too Far*, 1977) and lately Olivier has taken to admitting in interviews that he is making films more for his still-young children's bank balances than his own sense of pride as an actor.

'As long as I can stand', Olivier has said, 'I'll go on doing my job'. Even after a decade in which his physical health has been tested to the uttermost by three crippling illnesses it remains impossible to think of him in total retirement. Joan Plowright, his third wife and the mother of his three younger children (there is an elder son by Jill Esmond), once said that she somehow could not visualize her husband in an orchard working on his memoirs, and he added that he knew of no greater pleasure in life than setting off to work each morning and looking back over his shoulder to see the children waving from the window.

Other men already past their seventieth

Filmography
1930 Too Many Crooks; The Temporary Widow (GB–GER). '31 Potiphar's Wife (USA: Her Strange Desire); Friends and Lovers (USA); The Yellow Ticket (USA). '32 Westward Passage (USA). '33 Perfect Understanding; No Funny Business. '35 Moscow Nights (USA: I Stand Condemned). '36 As You Like It. '37 Fire Over England; 21 Days (USA: 21 Days Together). '38 The Divorce of Lady X. '39 Q Planes (USA: Clouds Over Europe); Wuthering Heights (USA). '40 Rebecca (USA); Conquest of the Air; Pride and Prejudice (USA). '41 Words for Battle (narr. only) (short); That Hamilton Woman! (USA) (GB: Lady Hamilton); 49th Parallel (USA: The Invaders). '43 The Demi-Paradise (USA: Adventure for Two). '44 Henry V (+dir; +prod; +co-sc). '48 Hamlet (+dir; +prod). '51 The Magic Box. '52 Carrie (USA). '53 A Queen Is Crowned (narr. only) (doc); The Beggar's Opera. '56 Richard III (+dir; +prod). '57 The Prince and the Showgirl (+dir; +co-prod). '59 The Devil's Disciple. '60 The Entertainer; Spartacus (USA). '61 The Power and the Glory (USA). '62 Term of Trial. '63 Uncle Vanya. '65 Bunny Lake Is Missing; Othello. '66 Khartoum. '68 Romeo and Juliet (narr. only) (GB-IT); The Shoes of the Fishermen (USA). '69 Oh! What a Lovely War; The Dance of Death; Battle of Britain; David Copperfield. '70 Three Sisters (+dir). '71 Nicholas and Alexandra. '72 Lady Caroline Lamb (GB-IT). '73 Sleuth. '75 Love Among the Ruins* (USA). '76 Marathon Man (USA); The Seven-Per-Cent Solution (USA). '77 A Bridge Too Far. '78 The Betsy (USA); The Boys From Brazil (USA). '79 A Little Romance (USA-FR); Dracula (USA).
* shot as TV film but shown in cinemas

The Evergreen Gregory Peck

Gregory Peck's integrity, dignity and sincerity have always brought him success, particularly during the Fifties when the threat of a nuclear holocaust gave Hollywood a new range of material

He was born in La Jolla, California, in 1916, and after finishing High School he enrolled at San Diego State College with the idea of pleasing his father by becoming a surgeon. However, finding that medicine didn't appeal he dropped out. A year or so later he entered the University of California at Berkeley and there he discovered his interest in drama.

The sideshows at the New York World Fair gave Peck his first taste of 'showbusiness'. His break, however, came while he was working as a Radio City guide, with a scholarship to the Neighborhood Playhouse School of the Theater, which was very keen on promoting promising young actors and actresses.

Peck began making his way in summer stock companies. Then in 1941 he made a screen test for David O. Selznick, who commented to one of his talent scouts that he didn't see how they could use Peck, and thought that most studios would have similar problems as he photographed like Abraham Lincoln and had little apparent personality. However, Broadway was not proving as successful as Peck might have hoped and he signed for the screenwriter Casey Robinson's short-lived production company, well aware of his limitations, and eager to learn his craft:

'On my first film, *Days of Glory* (1944), [Jacques] Tourneur taught me something I had to learn. He would criticise my precise diction and say "Common it up." . . . the microphone was just a few yards away, and I didn't need to project.'

Days of Glory, in which Peck played the leader of a Russian guerrilla group, was not a box-office success, but audiences came away with the memory of a large, loose-limbed actor with the gaunt, bony features that are a cameraman's delight – raw, a little awkward but unmistakeably an actor. Even then there was in his screen playing a hint of the quality that separates the artists from the players.

During Peck's theatrical days the Leland Hayward Agency had represented him. With new interest being shown in their property by Hollywood, Hayward set up a shrewd multi-package deal, contracting Peck to four companies over a six year period with a commitment to make 12 films. This enabled him to ring the changes on his image without being typecast or having to undergo the slow build-up to stardom in one studio's vehicles. In short succession Peck was a priest; a romantic lead opposite Ingrid Bergman and Greer Garson; a rakish, despicable but irresistible heavy; a stern but loving father; a big-game hunter; a barrister besotted with his client; a reporter experiencing anti-Semitism; a Western gun-fighter, and a wartime bomber-squadron commander. He emerged as a highly bankable star, carefully tailoring his talent to the projection of the quintessential Hemingway hero, displaying pride without vanity, forcefulness without

Below: Peck and William Wyler in front of the star-laden cast of The Big Country. *From left: Alfonso Bedoya, Charles Bickford, Jean Simmons, Charlton Heston, Carroll Baker, Burl Ives and Chuck Connors. Right: Peck sensitively portrayed the father of a son who loves a deer in* The Yearling *(1946)*

brutality and passion without sentimentality.

Popular literary and stage successes provided the core of Peck's work, and by 1951 David O. Selznick had revised his judgment:

'Peck we know to be the new rage, and if any further proof were needed, it was to be found in what happened at the previews of *Spellbound* (1945). We could not keep the audience quiet from the time his name first came on the screen until we had shushed the audience through three or four sequences, and stopped all the dames from "ohing" and "ahing" and gurgling.'

Serious roles – like the reporter posing as a Jew in *Gentleman's Agreement* (1947), who is sceptical of his assignment to investigate anti-Semitism because he feels it is none too apparent in its most blatant form, and assumes the manifestations are too subtle for non-Jewish folk to comprehend – authenticated the impression of dignity and intelligence. These were complemented by his roles for veteran director Henry King, as the martinet commander in *Twelve O'Clock High* (1949) and as *The Gunfighter* (1950) trying to live down his past reputation. They were exceptional in that they were 'character' roles, divested of glamour and sentimentality, projecting him as a loner – although the former was flawed by the insubstantial position the script takes on the moral nature of the task he is performing.

From 1950 Peck freelanced, always the star of the show and maintaining a strictly private life off-screen. However, in talking about his career he projects a slight insecurity – especially after one of his films fails – claiming that he doesn't think he is dull, just undemonstrative, and that his emotions are constantly being wrung by his work. Nevertheless, his choice of scripts has not always been sound. In *David and Bathsheba* (1951), for instance, Peck's David grew into a credible individual – proud,

Filmography
1944 Days of Glory; The Keys of the Kingdom. '45 The Valley of Decision; Spellbound. '46 The Yearling; Duel in the Sun. '47 The Macomber Affair; Gentleman's Agreement; The Paradine Case. '48 Yellow Sky. '49 The Great Sinner; Twelve O'Clock High. '50 The Gunfighter. '51 Only the Valiant; Captain Horatio Hornblower (GB: Captain Horatio Hornblower RN). '51 David and Bathsheba. '52 The World in His Arms. '53 The Snows of Kilimanjaro; Roman Holiday. '54 The Million Pound Note (USA: Man With a Million) (GB); Night People. '55 The Purple Plain. '56 The Man in the Gray Flannel Suit; Moby Dick. '57 Designing Woman. '58 The Big Country

anguished, with a wry streak of humour and the recognizable vices and virtues of most human beings – but much depended on Peck's strength of portrayal to rise above the short-comings of the script. Equally, *Night People* (1954) – about an exchange of political prisoners in Berlin – fails to convince because of the hysterical anti-Red feeling it portrays.

Gregory Peck is a very methodical worker, writing notes on his scripts and asking himself questions as a means of finding his way into a character. After his first three or four pictures he used to sit in on story conferences and make helpful comments. Sometimes his suggestions were accepted and he was soon allowed to approve the director, co-star and script for his films. Sheilah Graham was Scott Fitzgerald's mistress during the last depressing years of the author's life and was dismayed at 20th Century-Fox's portrayal of their affair in *Beloved Infidel* (1959). She cited a number of instances in which Peck's extraordinary insistence on being so involved with the production reflected a concern less for the film itself than for his being the star of the show. During the filming of *Beloved Infidel* Graham commented on her memory of the moment when she realized that Scott had begun drinking again: '"Oh, no," said Greg, "I don't see it like that. I'll say something pleasant and smile."'

Graham also notes that Peck took his status very seriously:

'As a tax advantage, Greg co-produced *The Big Country* (1958) with Willie Wyler directing. As in most of these deals, Greg's co-producership was more of an honorary title . . . Wyler will not take interference from anyone. There was a close-up and Greg wanted it one way and Willie wanted it his way. After some arguing the star drew himself up to his over six feet and said: "I'm the producer." "Shit", replied Wyler. They didn't speak to each other for years.'

A serious-minded man, Peck is politically active as a Democrat and is a successful fundraiser for the Motion Picture Relief Fund and the Building and Endowment Campaign. As a former president of the Academy of Motion Picture Arts and Sciences his most spectacular

Above: based on a real event in Korea, Pork Chop Hill *(1959) starred Peck as the colonel in command of an attack on a hill that was of questionable strategic value. Below left: Ava Gardner and Peck in* On the Beach. *Below: Peck, as Atticus Finch, guards his jailed client in* To Kill a Mockingbird

(+co-prod). '59 Pork Chop Hill (+prod); Beloved Infidel. '60 On the Beach. '61 The Guns of Navarone (GB). '62 Cape Fear; To Kill a Mockingbird; How the West Was Won. '63 Captain Newman MD. '64 Behold a Pale Horse. '65 Mirage. '66 John F. Kennedy: Years of Lightning, Day of Drums (doc) (narr only); Arabesque. '68 The Stalking Moon. '69 MacKenna's Gold; The Chairman (GB: The Most Dangerous Man in the World); Marooned. '70 I Walk the Line. '71 Shootout. '72 The Trial of the Catonsville Nine (prod only). '74 Billy Two Hats; The Dove (prod only). '76 The Omen. '77 MacArthur (GB: Mac-Arthur the Rebel General). '78 The Boys from Brazil. '80 The Sea Wolves.

achievement, in the civic field, came after Dr Martin Luther King's assassination five days before the Oscar ceremony in 1968. All the coloured presenters withdrew, and the following day Peck decided to postpone the ceremony until after the funeral – the only time the awards have ever been delayed. He convinced the NBC, the sponsors and the performers to fall in line and this persuasive dignity and sincerity are the cornerstones of his two best performances: *On the Beach* (1960) and *To Kill a Mockingbird* (1962).

In *On the Beach* – as the commander of a nuclear submarine which survives the Bomb by being submerged – Peck gave a powerful performance. His wife and children having died when the Bomb dropped, the commander heads for Australia as the Southern Hemisphere has temporarily escaped contamination. He falls in love with an attractive woman – played by Ava Gardner – but although they enjoy each other's company he finally decides to return to America so his men can die on home ground. In *To Kill a Mockingbird* – for which he won an Oscar – he plays Atticus Finch, a small-town lawyer defending a negro, quietly courageous, sharp in business but tender and loving towards his children. The action of the film is counterpointed by the elegiac recollection of childhood and the portrait of a very human father dedicated to the pursuit of truth and justice.

During the late Sixties and the Seventies Peck appeared less frequently, turning to the production of the controversial *The Trial of the Catonsville Nine* (1972) – which dealt with the sensitive political issue of Vietnam – and the vapid *The Dove* (1974):

'It wouldn't have been my wish to go on making three or four films a year as I did for so many years, but, on the other hand, I'm not offered as many as when I was say 35. That's natural, and I knew that time would come. I've no feeling of regret about it.'

He has continued to pick varied roles, reviving his career by playing the American ambassador to Britain in the highly successful horror film, *The Omen* (1976) – who else could have made such a role believable? He followed this with a portrayal of the Nazi doctor, Mengele, in the fictionalized biography *The*

Top: I Walk the Line (1970) was not a box-office success but Peck's performance as the sheriff, who ruins himself by falling for the daughter of a moonshiner, is moving. Left: Peck as MacArthur (1977). *Below: Deborah Raffin, Joseph Bottoms and Peck the producer during filming of* The Dove

Boys from Brazil (1978).

When asked about his tremendous scope he explains that most of his characters are not close to his own personality – giving *Duel in the Sun* (1946), in which he was a rascal, a rich man's spoiled son, as an example. But in the main he plays heroes who are beset by difficulties imposed upon them by circumstances beyond their control or by 'evil' people. Arguably the less pleasant characters have stretched him, and are more memorable than roles such as the journalist in *Roman Holiday* (1953), who falls in love with a runaway princess, or the businessman in *The Man in the Gray Flannel Suit* (1956), where the moral is that the acquisition of power and wealth is not necessarily desirable.

Peck sees his talent for communicating sincerity as an expression of his concentration. As the film historian and biographer Tony Thomas has noted, he projects his own integrity in his work:

'The image is that of a good man. It may not be a terribly exciting or stimulating image but in its strength and in its implied virtues it is an image of value, particularly for Americans.'

KINGSLEY CANHAM

Uphill racer
Robert Redford

TV star, sex-symbol, superstar. In just twenty years Robert Redford has achieved star status by successfully combining all three attributes, but at the peak of his profession he seems to be forging himself a new career, this time in the field of direction

With his blond hair, blue eyes and clean-cut all-American appearance, Robert Redford seems to be perfectly cast as a star in the grand Hollywood tradition of the male romantic lead. Nevertheless, Redford's emotional entanglements have usually been subsidiary to the main plot of his films: with the exceptions of Barbra Streisand and Jane Fonda he has rarely played opposite actresses of equal calibre. Indeed, some would argue that his only screen love affair has been with Paul Newman.

The films that work best are those in which there is a quiet questioning of the stereotyped American male, and which thereby gently subvert Redford's own pretty-boy image. He has attacked the notion of the attractive athletic winner – *Downhill Racer* (1969), *Little Fauss and Big Halsy* (1970). *The Electric Horseman* (1979) – commented on the heroic legends of the Hollywood West – *Butch Cassidy and the Sundance Kid, Tell Them Willie Boy Is Here* (both 1969), *Jeremiah Johnson* (1972) – and played the naive American caught up in somebody else's politics – *The Candidate* (1972), *The Way We Were* (1973), *Three Days of the Condor* (1975), *All the President's Men* (1976).

The cream on its way to the top

Redford's early life was not that of the well-to-do middle-class American that his appearance would seem to suggest. Born in 1937, the son of a milkman, Redford grew up in Santa Monica, California, in the shadow of the 'dream factory' itself. But he despised the movies, often shouting at the screen on visits to the cinema with his friends. Despite rebelling against the discipline of school, he won a baseball scholarship to the University of Colorado, but soon dropped out, believing there was more to life than sport. After hitch-hiking around various European capitals, painting, and 'loitering' in bars and cafés, he returned to America to study art at New York's Pratt Institute, and eventually found himself at the American Academy of Dramatic Arts. He had several minor roles on Broadway before the breakthrough came – the lead part in Neil Simon's domestic farce *Barefoot in the Park*. The play, directed by Mike Nichols, had rave reviews and Redford earned recognition for his comic ability. With a growing reputation on television, it was not surprising that he was soon much sought after by Hollywood.

Skimming the heights

However, his first film, *War Hunt* (1962), was a second-rate, low-budget venture about a psychotic private in Korea. It was not a great success for either its producers or Redford, but during the filming he met and struck up a long working relationship with the then actor Sydney Pollack – who later directed several of Redford's films. Redford's career continued with *Inside Daisy Clover* (1965), the film version of Gavin Lambert's novel about the machinations of Hollywood. He then went on to make a total flop, *Situation Hopeless, But Not Serious* (1965); turned in a highly praised performance as Bubber Reeves, the escaped convict whose presence brings out the mercenary tendencies of his home-town folk in *The Chase* (1966); starred with Natalie Wood in a Tennessee Williams' small-town melodrama, *This Property Is Condemned* (1966); and was sued by Paramount for walking out on the Western *Blue* (1968) (a wise decision on his part since the completed film, starring Terence Stamp, was not a success).

In 1967 he returned to Hollywood to fulfil an obligation to film *Barefoot in the Park*. Echoing his stage success, Redford's role as Paul Bratter, the straitlaced lawyer whose new wife (Jane Fonda) complains about his lack of spontaneity – he cannot even walk barefoot in the park – swept him to fame. Although Redford disliked Bratter's image he found a niche for himself as the fall-guy to his more active partner and he and Fonda made an

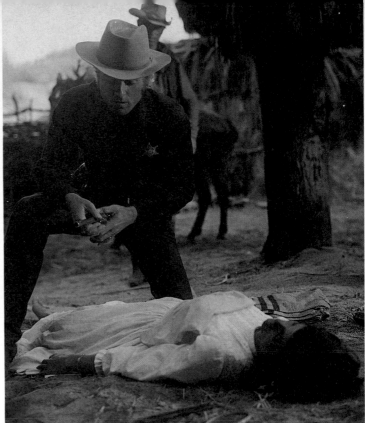

Opposite page: Redford with Gene Hackman, skiing champion and coach in Downhill Racer (left), and with Natalie Wood and the director Sydney Pollack filming This Property is Condemned (right). Left: Michael J. Pollard and Redford as Little Fauss and Big Halsy

Above left: Redford as Paul Bratter who drunkenly loses his inhibitions in Barefoot in the Park. Above: Sheriff Cooper finds his quarry's fiancée (Katharine Ross) dead in Tell Them Willie Boy Is Here. Below: Jeremiah Johnson with Bear Claw (Will Geer)

effervescent duo.

Redford was subsequently offered several major roles which he turned down – including the diffident Benjamin in *The Graduate* (1967). It was well worth the wait for 1969 was Redford's year – he had a critical success with *Tell Them Willie Boy Is Here*, made his long-cherished project *Downhill Racer*, and after Marlon Brando, Steve McQueen and Warren Beatty had all dropped out of the running he was offered what will probably remain his most memorable role, that of the Sundance Kid in *Butch Cassidy and the Sundance Kid*. The attractive vitality of the relationship between the two heroes, and their tongue-in-cheek humour, made the film a smash hit. Redford may not say much in the film, but his laconic, fast-shooting Sundance Kid complemented Newman's thoughtful Butch. The male camaraderie and slick repartee encouraged the quick growth of buddy-buddy movies and four years later Newman and Redford were reunited on

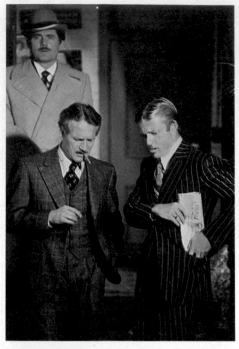

Far left: the partners in crime (Paul Newman and Redford) act out their charade in front of the victim (Robert Shaw) in The Sting. *Left: a man with a past to hide – Redford as* The Great Gatsby. *Below left: as Bob Woodward in* All the President's Men.

the screen in *The Sting* (1973). Once again under the direction of George Roy Hill, it is a witty story concerning a successful confidence trick on a racketeer. It was another hit.

How the West was

Butch Cassidy and the Sundance Kid made Redford a valuable property and enabled him to pick and choose his parts. Having deserted Hollywood for the mountains of Utah and a commitment to ecological preservation, many of his films comment on the values he left behind, with a recurrent theme being the false heroics of the Western. *Tell Them Willie Boy Is Here*, with Abraham Polonsky making a return to direction after years on the blacklist, tackles the treatment of the American Indians. Redford was originally offered the part of Willie Boy – the Paiute Indian who kills a chief while claiming his bride and finds himself hunted as a renegade – but, feeling that Indian roles should be played by Indians, he opted for the role of Sheriff Cope who learns to respect the Indian traditions. *Jeremiah Johnson*, a legendary story of a lone trapper who braves the elements to live his own life in the mountains, is another film that challenges Hollywood's heroic notions. Redford's Johnson is neither braver nor wiser than others: he is simply more determined to live free from interference. In a totally different setting, the wealthy Twenties as depicted by Scott Fitzgerald in *The Great Gatsby* (1974), Redford portrays another loner who rejects 'modern' society's materialism. However, the film failed because it was one of the few Redford films that indulged itself as a love story.

Redford has expressed his dislike of the born competitor who smiles as he clocks up the wins and the girls:

'What about the athlete who is a creep? We do tend to tolerate creeps if they win. They can behave any way so just forget that swell guy whom everyone loves and who came second.'

With 20,000 feet of unofficial footage from the Grenoble Winter Olympics, and after a two-year struggle, Redford was finally able to embody these views in *Downhill Racer* – a couple of seasons in the life of David Chappellet, a skier who is only admired so long as he keeps winning. That Redford's looks made it difficult to believe Chappellet is such a jerk

Filmography
1962 War Hunt. '65 Situation Hopeless, But Not Serious; Inside Daisy Clover. '66 The Chase; This Property Is Condemned. '67 Barefoot in the Park. '69 Butch Cassidy and the Sundance Kid; Tell Them Willie Boy Is Here; Downhill Racer. '70 The Making of Butch Cassidy and the Sundance Kid; Little Fauss and Big Halsy. '72 The Hot Rock (GB: How to Steal a Diamond in Four Uneasy Lessons); Jeremiah Johnson; The Candidate (+co-exec. prod.). '73 The Way We Were; The Sting. '74 The Great Gatsby; Broken Treaty at Battle Mountain (doc) (narr. only). '75 The Great Waldo Pepper; Three Days of the Condor. '76 All the President's Men (+co-exec. prod.). '77 A Bridge Too Far. '79 The Electric Horseman. '80 Brubaker; Ordinary People (dir. only).

emphasizes the very point the film is trying to make. *Little Fauss and Big Halsy* develops the same theme, this time on the motorcycle racetrack. The misguided admiration that Fauss (Michael J. Pollard) holds for his more confident fellow competitor Halsy (Redford) leads only to disillusionment. However, the most revealing image of the American athletic winner is in *The Electric Horseman*; the drunken, ex-rodeo champion rides out of town on the prize horse he has rescued from the breakfast-cereal company he publicizes. All that can be seen of him against the night is his illuminated outline – a visual indication of the hollowness of that kind of success.

A man for the people

Several of Redford's films have examined the manipulations and threats of modern politics: in *The Way We Were*, the McCarthy witch-hunt is the cause of the break-up of a young Hollywood couple's marriage when the wife Katie (Barbra Streisand) becomes involved in the campaign against the blacklist; *The Candidate* looks at competition in the electoral fight as a certain-to-loose well-intentioned contender (Redford) becomes seduced by the political arena; *Three Days of the Condor* is a spy thriller about a desk-worker for the CIA who, on returning to his office, finds all his colleagues shot dead, possibly by his own side; *Brubaker* (1980) investigates the clash of interests between a prison governor bent on reform and the corrupt local businessmen and politicians.

But undoubtedly Redford's major intervention into political film is *All the President's Men*. He had negotiated a film deal with Woodward and Bernstein even before the book of the Watergate cover-up investigation had been written. He then spent a long time researching the journalistic background by talking to the reporters and staff of the *Washington Post*. The resulting film – with Dustin Hoffman and Redford as the two intrepid reporters – is a strong indictment of power politics and the distortions which ensue.

Bridging the gap

Despite being one of Hollywood's highest-paid stars – he commanded a fee of $2 million for 20 days work on *A Bridge Too Far* (1977) – he declined to appear in his directorial debut, *Ordinary People* (1980). It is a highly emotional and perceptive study of family tensions based upon the guilt that the son Conrad (Tim Hutton) feels over his brother's drowning. When talking about his brother's death Conrad is unable to express his feelings and wonders what John Boy – of the popular television series *The Waltons* – would have said, an astute observation of the powerful effect America's 'heroes' have on ordinary lives. But at the end of the film, when the mother (Mary Tyler Moore) has gone away leaving husband (Donald Sutherland) and son contented together, it is interesting to note that Redford still seems to be perpetuating the male-orientated world of *Butch Cassidy and the Sundance Kid*.
SALLY HIBBIN

Left: Redford played a small role in A Bridge Too Far, *the story of the Allied defeat at Arnhem. Above right: an ex-rodeo rider decides to leave the bright lights behind in* The Electric Horseman. *Right: Redford discusses a scene from* Ordinary People *with Donald Sutherland*

Edward G. Robinson

Robinson as Rico down on his luck in Little Caesar *(left), as a scientist in* Dr Ehrlich's Magic Bullet *(above), a framed businessman in* Blackmail *(1939, above right) and a jaded lawyer in* Illegal *(1955, far right)*

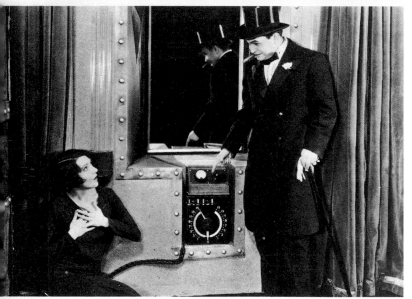

Edward G. Robinson, describing the opening of one of his earlier speeches while entertaining the troops during World War II, wrote in his autobiography:

'I began by saying: "I am happy to be here, the most privileged moment of my life, to see the men who are defeating Hitler." . . . I could sense the audience despising me . . . and to stop the buzz of their boos and Bronx cheers, I ad-libbed, "Pipe down, you mugs, or I'll let you have it. Whaddya hear from the mob?" There was an instant burst of high laughter and applause.'

Throughout his book Robinson returns obsessively to a fact that he found incomprehensible; people knew him and wanted to see him primarily as Rico, the title figure in his famous 1930 film *Little Caesar*. The reasons why he found this so surprising have partly to do with

cultural attitudes as to what is important in art – in particular the debate about whether High Art is to be preferred to Popular Art – but in Robinson's case the reasons go deeper. They relate to the time and place in which he was born and raised.

Born Emanuel Goldenberg on December 12, 1893 in Bucharest, Romania, Robinson's family background was based on Jewish discipline and middle-class values. At that time the Jews were denied civil rights in Romania and were subjected to periodic persecution, an important factor in the emigration of the family to the United States in the early years of the century. The moral tone of the Goldenberg family was akin to a certain brand of Protestantism which stressed morality and hard work. However, the Goldenberg family was slightly unorthodox, having a European predisposition

Above left: with Claudette Colbert in The Hole in the Wall *(1929), one of Robinson's earliest gangster roles. Above:* East is West *(1930) featured Lupe Velez and Robinson as an unlikely Chinese pair*

to a highly romantic conception of art.

These elements would have, of themselves, inclined the young Robinson to be hostile to the cinema as a mass art – which was indeed to be the case – but they were reinforced by his choice of career as a theatre actor. During the Twenties Robinson rose to become a considerable figure on the Broadway stage, appearing in a whole range of classic and modern plays and deciding early on that because of his appearance his future was as a character actor rather than as a leading man.

It is often assumed that *Little Caesar* was

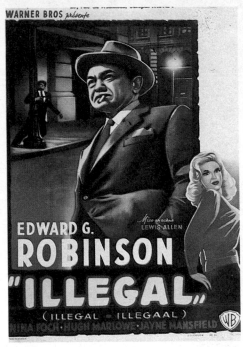

A Master of his Art

Above: in danger of being typecast. Robinson played a corrupt gangster figure in Barbary Coast *(1935). Above right: a scornful Kitty (Joan Bennett) makes use of her besotted admirer (Robinson) in* Scarlet Street

Robinson's first picture but his stage reputation ensured that he had received offers to go to Hollywood from the early Twenties. The handful of movies he made before *Little Caesar* confirmed for him his intuitive dislike of the medium. Characteristically, while appearing in a theatrical production of *Peer Gynt* he stole off to see himself in his first film, the silent *The Bright Shawl* (1923) – in which he played a Spanish aristocrat – and was appalled.

Little Caesar is regarded as the first of the classic gangster movies and Rico, the Italian immigrant whose rise and fall the film charts,

the first of the classic gangster 'heroes' – even to the extent of his lying dead in the street at the end of the film. Robinson never understood its success and his remarks on the film sought to make analogies with Greek tragedy as a way of explaining its popularity:

'He (Rico) is a man who defies society, and in the end is mowed down by the gods and society, and doesn't even know what happened . . . the picture has sustained itself throughout these years because it was constructed as a Greek tragedy.'

His upbringing and training made it impossible for him to appreciate the virtues of pace, simplicity, action and contemporaneity.

The paradox is that Robinson became a complete master of the art of screen acting while at the same time regarding most of his film work as beneath contempt. Understand-

ably he was to play in several gangster films as a contract player with Warner Brothers during the Thirties, but he always aspired to roles which approximated more to his conception of 'good theatre'.

He always regarded his finest role as that of Paul Ehrlich – the man who discovered a cure for syphilis – in *Dr Ehrlich's Magic Bullet* (1940) perhaps because of the manifest seriousness of the project. It is significant that the aggressive, lower-class hoodlums he played in the Thirties tended to give way, in the mid-Forties, to articulate bourgeois figures as in *Double Indemnity* (1944), in which he played a shrewd insurance investigator, *Woman in the Window* (1944), which featured him as a psychology professor, *Scarlet Street* (1945), in which he was a clerk who finds in painting an escape from the oppression of the *petit bourgeois*

of Impressionist pictures and was a considerable painter in his own right, as well as being a confidant of the most illustrious musical figures in America.

If his European background inclined him to an elitist and rather conservative view of art, it predisposed him to an egalitarian and progressive view of politics. Throughout the Thirties and early Forties he lent his name, time and money to a number of progressive causes, a fact which was to cost him dearly during the infamous anti-communist witch-hunts of the late Forties and early Fifties. Though not remotely a communist himself, Robinson's affinity with democratic ideals got him blacklisted for a time.

This and his own early commitment to 'character' roles, meant that his later career was as a supporting actor of great eminence, range and distinction. The more 'theatrical' side of his persona was perhaps best shown in his playing of the temperamental film director in *Two Weeks in Another Town* (1962) and the 'cinematic' side in his role as ace poker player in *The Cincinnati Kid* (1965). There was more than some truth in his final remark to Steve McQueen in the latter: 'As long as I'm around, you're second best; you may as well learn to live with it.'　　　　　　COLIN McARTHUR

Above left: The Kid (Steve McQueen) and The Man (Robinson), rivals at the poker table in The Cincinatti Kid. *Below: Robinson as an accomplice in the theft of a statue from St Peter's, Rome, in* Operazione San Pietro *(1968, Operation St Peter's). Below right: with Raquel Welch on the set of* The Biggest Bundle of Them All *(1967)*

milieu in which he lives and works, and *All My Sons* (1948), in which he played a man selling defective airplane parts to the government.

At the same time Robinson seems to have had an odd blindness and lack of sympathy for *Scarlet Street*, given its critical importance as a major film by Fritz Lang and the closeness of its theme – a Sunday painter who produces masterpieces – to an important dimension of his own life. In the debate about High Art or Popular Art Robinson was firmly on the side of High Art. He had built up a renowned collection

Filmography

1923 The Bright Shawl. '29 The Hole in the Wall. '30 Night Ride; A Lady to Love; Outside the Law; East is West; The Widow from Chicago; Little Caesar. '31 Smart Money; Five Star Final. '32 The Stolen Jools (short) (GB: The Slippery Pearls); The Hatchet Man (GB: The Honourable Mr Wong); Two Seconds; Tiger Shark; Silver Dollar. '33 The Little Giant; I Loved a Woman; Dark Hazard. '34 The Man With Two Faces. '35 The Whole Town's Talking (GB: Passport to Fame); A Day at Santa Anita (short) (guest); Barbary Coast. '36 Bullets or Ballots. '37 Thunder in the City (GB); Kid Galahad; The Last Gangster. '38 A Slight Case of Murder; The Amazing Dr Clitterhouse; I Am the Law. '39 Confessions of a Nazi Spy; Blackmail. '40 Dr Ehrlich's Magic Bullet (GB: The Story of Dr Ehrlich's Magic Bullet); Brother Orchid; A Dispatch From Reuters (GB: This Man Reuter); Manpower. '41 The Sea Wolf; Unholy Partners. '42 Moscow Strikes Back (doc) (narr only); Tales of Manhattan; Larceny Inc. '43 The Red Cross at War (doc) (narr only); Projection of America (doc) (on-screen narr only); Destroyer; Flesh and Fantasy; Screen Snapshots, Series 22, No 4 (short) (compere only). '44 Tampico; Screen Snapshots, Series 23, No 9 (short) (guest); Double Indemnity; Mr Winkle Goes to War (GB: Arms and the Woman); The Woman in the Window. '45 Our Vines Have Tender Grapes; Journey Together (GB); Scarlet Street. '46 The Stranger. '47 The Red House. '48 All My Sons; Where Do You Get Off? (short) (narr only); Key Largo; Night Has a Thousand Eyes. '49 House of Strangers; It's a Great Feeling (guest). '50 My Daughter Joy (GB) (USA: Operation X); Screen Snapshots (short). '52 Actors and Sin *ep* Actor's Blood. '53 Vice Squad (GB: The Girl in Room 17); Big Leaguer; The Glass Web. '54 Black Tuesday; The Violent Men (GB: Rough Company). '55 Tight Spot; A Bullet for Joey; Illegal; Hell on Frisco Bay. '56 Nightmare; The Ten Commandments. '57 The Heart of Show Business (doc) (co-narr only). '59 A Hole in the Head; Israel (doc) (narr only). '60 Seven Thieves; Pepe (guest). '61 My Geisha. '62 Two Weeks in Another Town. '63 Sammy Going South (GB) (USA: A Boy Ten Feet Tall); The Prize. '64 Good Neighbour Sam; Robin and the Seven Hoods (guest); The Outrage; Cheyenne Autumn. '65 The Cincinnati Kid; Who Has Seen the Wind? (United Nations). '67 Le Blonde de Pekin (FR-IT-GER) (USA: Peking Blonde); The Biggest Bundle of Them All (USA-IT); Ad Ogni Costa (IT-SP-GER) (USA/GB: Grand Slam). '68 Never a Dull Moment; Operazione San Pietro (IT-FR-GER); Uno Scacco tutto Matto (IT-SP). '69 Mackenna's Gold. '70 Song of Norway. '72 Neither by Day or Night (USA-IS); Soylent Green.

Mr Stewart Goes to Hollywood

As the all-American Mr Average, James Stewart has been loved and admired for over four decades. A family man of spotless repute, he has built his career on just such an image. However, in recent years he has displayed an intriguing versatility and revelled in roles revealing the darker side of his nature

Above left: James Stewart as the famous bandleader in The Glenn Miller Story. *Top: Jefferson Smith (Stewart) and his secretary (Jean Arthur) discuss the attractions of the capital in* Mr Smith Goes to Washington. *Above: as Elwood P. Dowd he tries to explain that 'the rabbit just left' in* Harvey

It is possible that no star ever had a better run of pictures than James Stewart did in the four years between 1937 and 1940. There was *Seventh Heaven* (1937), *You Can't Take It With You* (1938), *Mr Smith Goes to Washington*, *Destry Rides Again* (both 1939), *The Shop Around the Corner* and *The Philadelphia Story* (both 1940). It was in these films that his basic screen character – the gulpy voice, gangling walk and sweet, yet principled spirit – was established. His billing might ever be *James Stewart* but he indelibly remains *Jimmy*, the friendly and somehow reassuring diminuative recalling his small-town origins and reiterating his continuing responsibility for personifying the simpler values of a simpler American time.

However, if those films – climaxed in 1946, after a gap in his career for war service, by Capra's cult classic, *It's a Wonderful Life* – established his image, they did not establish his credentials as an actor. That came later, some years after the war, when he self-consciously set about changing his image. *It's a Wonderful Life* was Capra's marvellously sentimental tribute to the verities of American small-town life but was not a success when released, and neither was Stewart's next film, *Magic Town*

(1947). It was obvious that at 34, with a distinguished military record behind him, Stewart was both too old chronologically and too mature emotionally to go on playing juveniles. As he himself put it, too many of the reviews were saying things like: 'Jimmy Stewart is still exuding boyish charm in lethal doses.'

From soft centre to tough nut

He began the process of change in *Call Northside 777* (1948), in which he played a tough but principled Chicago police reporter devoted to clearing an innocent man of a murder charge. In the same year he began his salutary association with Alfred Hitchcock in *Rope*. Here he plays a teacher who comes to realize that his Nazi-like philosophy has led two of his students to motiveless murder. He is therefore obliged to uncover evidence not only of the crime, but also of his own intellectual complicity in it.

If these two films mark the beginning of a turn in Stewart's career, it was the incredible series of Westerns made with Anthony Mann between 1950 and 1955 that established him as an actor to be reckoned with. *Winchester '73* (1950), the story of a man searching for his

father's killer; *Bend of the River* (1952), with Stewart helping a group of pioneers to cross the West; *The Naked Spur* (1953), where he is a bounty hunter; *The Far Country* (1954), in which he plays a 'gritty' cowboy; *The Man From Laramie* (1955), which again sees him as a man out for vengeance – these are among the finest works in the genre. The vision retained of him in these films is of a man in a battered sheepskin jacket with several days stubble on his chin, riding off alone into the high country toward some confrontation – not only with the villain but with his own driving obsessions – that would be cold and lonely.

There was, as critic Jim Kitses has noted, something of the old Stewart in these roles. Mann used the 'charming, bemused side of the actor's talent' in order to make palatable his characters' cynicism and to soften their violent edges. There was also about Stewart a quality that has always endeared him to directors and co-workers – a capacity for disciplined hard work. In interviews Mann would speak admiringly of Stewart's willingness to undergo any hardship (fights were staged under the hooves of horses, the actor permitted himself to be dragged through fire) endure any learning process (he made himself an expert with the

Above: Stewart and Maureen Sullavan as the antagonistic shop assistants unaware that they are pen-pals in The Shop Around the Corner. *Above right: with Lee J. Cobb in the film that introduced a tougher image,* Call Northside 777. *Above, far right: as a trigger-happy cowboy in* The Far Country. *Right: as the peaceable part-time sheriff driven to violence in* Firecreek *(1968)*

Winchester rifle through dogged practice) in order to achieve the hard-bitten authenticity that marked these pictures.

By and large they were not expensively produced films, and in this period Stewart alternated his appearances in Westerns with work in more expensive and 'civilized' roles. Yet even in these there seemed to be an attempt by the actor to break his old mould. Occasionally the results were ludicrous – as when he appeared in DeMille's *The Greatest Show on Earth* (1951) as a clown who never dared take off his makeup in case the police should recognize him as a wanted criminal. Sometimes they were merely bland and conventional, as in such biopics as *The Stratton Story* (1949), the life of baseball star Monty Stratton, and *The Glenn Miller Story* (1953); sometimes they were routinely heroic, as in *Strategic Air Command* (1955), in which Stewart was a Lieutenant-Colonel in the US peacetime air force, and *The FBI Story* (1959), the career of an FBI agent through 25 years of service. However, whether ludicrous, bland or routine, they were still very popular and Stewart was often high on the end-of-year exhibitors' list of leading box-office draws.

Days of wine and rabbits

These years also produced much that was far from ordinary. *Harvey* (1950) was the story of Elwood P. Dowd, a gentle alcoholic who has an imaginary rabbit for a companion. Stewart had already appeared in the role on stage in 1947 (and was to return to a stage production in later years) and in the movie he pushed his slight air of befuddlement, always present in

his early portrayals, to epic – yet delicately stated – proportions. Or what about his two finest Hitchcock roles? As the magazine photographer confined to his room by a broken leg in *Rear Window* (1954), Stewart is as sweetly engaging as ever. But he is also, never forget, that unsavoury figure, a dedicated voyeur. In *Vertigo* (1958) he plays a detective not only somewhat unmanned by his fear of heights but obsessed – to the point of derangement by a lost love. Then there was *Anatomy of a Murder* (1959) in which, at first glance, he seems to be playing the grown-up version of one of his old small-town kids until we begin to sense – under all his gargling, gawking and shuffling about – a steely and stubborn mind at work, serving as his own private detective in order to uncover evidence of his client's innocence. That mind is unsheathed in the courtroom sequences where it works fast and tough to best his legal opponent, a big-city prosecutor played by George C. Scott.

The man from Indiana

There was a feeling during those years that 'Jimmy' was deceiving the public by encouraging it to believe that the man it saw was simply the man he was. Certainly what was known of his private life was exemplary. There was never, in the endlessly gossiping Hollywood press, the slightest note of indecorousness. He married late, aged 41, but it was to be a lasting relationship and in 1951 his wife Gloria produced twins. During World War II he had risen from Private to Colonel in the air force and received, among other decorations, the Distinguished Flying Cross for his 23 bombing missions over Germany; after the war he persisted in his military duties, rising in the Reserve to the rank of General. In politics Stewart has always been a conservative Republican, though never strident about it, and has maintained a friendship with Henry Fonda, a determined liberal – which dates back to the time when they were both 'novice'

actors with the University Players theatre group in the early Thirties – precisely because they refuse to discuss politics. And Stewart went around saying, as he still does, that: 'the most important thing about acting is to approach it as a craft, not as an art and not as some mysterious type of religion.' He likes to tell reporters how lucky he was to have come up through the old studio system where young players were worked hard.

Be that as it may, there is something more than mere craft in all those quietly bent strangers, those oddly bedevilled and curiously possessed loners he kept playing. As Stewart got older the press took to calling him an elder statesman; however he did not spend all his time playing kindly uncles and grandpas. He is an out-and-out villain in *Bandolero!* (1968) as the crooked brother of a murderer, and in 1970 he was to be found playing a rancher who comes into some property – a whorehouse – with another old reprobate, played by Henry Fonda, in *The Cheyenne Social Club*. His last

Below: with Richard Attenborough, Christian Marquand and Hardy Kruger in Flight of the Phoenix *(1966), a story of desert endurance. Bottom: the new owner and his friend (Henry Fonda) take over* The Cheyenne Social Club

truly great role in *Fool's Parade* (1971) – about an old convict determined to have his revenge on the people who unjustly sent him to jail – is amazing. The convict has a glass eye which he pops out of its socket and talks to at times of stress, variously frightening or mesmerizing anyone who happens to be nearby. At the end of the picture he walks around with a coatful of dynamite, more than pleased to touch off the fuse and take his enemies along with him to kingdom come if they do not accede to his demands.

This is hardly the behaviour of an air force General, or of the nice middle-class boy born in 1908 whose father owned the hardware store in Indiana. Therefore, it is easy to suspect this model citizen of being a secret subversive, one of those actors who uses stage and screen to work off their private frets and passions, the better to return home and pretend that the job they've been doing all day at the studio is just an exercise in 'craft'.

In his maturity James Stewart has taken great pleasure in displaying his instinctive, brooding and occasionally depressive side. His ability to do so without destroying any affection for his innocent young men of the past has enabled him to make the most difficult of all movie transitions – from guiless juvenile to strong and knowledgeable leading man – without missing a stride. More recently this skill has allowed him to slip gracefully across the line from lead to character actor, and the range of his 'craft' can now be fully appreciated. However, he is perhaps really loved for his duplicity – his insistence that he is just an ordinary fellow.   RICHARD SCHICKEL

Filmography
1935 Murder Man. '36 Rose Marie; Next Time We Love (GB: Next Time We Live); Wife Versus Secretary; Small Town Girl; Speed; The Gorgeous Hussy; Born to Dance; After the Thin Man. '37 Seventh Heaven; The Last Gangster; Navy Blue and Gold. '38 Of Human Hearts; Vivacious Lady; You Can't Take It With You. '39 Made for Each Other; Ice Follies of 1939; It's a Wonderful World; Mr Smith Goes to Washington; Destry Rides Again. '40 The Shop Around the Corner; The Mortal Storm; No Time for Comedy; The Philadelphia Story. '41 Come Live With Me; Pot o' Gold (GB: The Golden Hour); Ziegfeld Girl. '46 The American Creed (short) (GB: American Brotherhood Week); It's a Wonderful Life. '47 Magic Town. '48 Call Northside 777; On Our Merry Way (preview title: A Miracle Can Happen); Rope; You Gotta Stay Happy. '49 The Stratton Story. '50 Malaya (GB: East of the Rising Sun); Winchester '73; Broken Arrow; The Jackpot; Harvey. '51 No Highway (USA: No Highway in the Sky) (GB); The Greatest Show on Earth. '52 Bend of the River (GB: Where the River Bends); Carbine Williams. '53 The Naked Spur; Thunder Bay; The Glenn Miller Story. '54 Rear Window; The Far Country. '55 Strategic Air Command; The Man From Laramie. '56 The Man Who Knew Too Much. '57 The Spirit of St Louis; Night Passage. '58 Vertigo; Bell, Book and Candle. '59 Anatomy of a Murder; The FBI Story. '60 Mountain Road. '61 Two Rode Together; X-15 (narration only). '62 The Man Who Shot Liberty Valance; Mr Hobbs Takes a Vacation; How the West Was Won. '63 Take Her, She's Mine. '64 Cheyenne Autumn. '65 Dear Brigitte; Shenandoah. '66 The Rare Breed; Flight of the Phoenix. '68 Firecreek; Bandolero!. '70 The Cheyenne Social Club. '71 Fools' Parade (GB: Dynamite Man from Glory Jail). '74 That's Entertainment! (co-narr). '76 The Shootist. '77 Airport '77; The Big Sleep. '78 The Magic of Lassie.

Spencer Tracy
the face of integrity

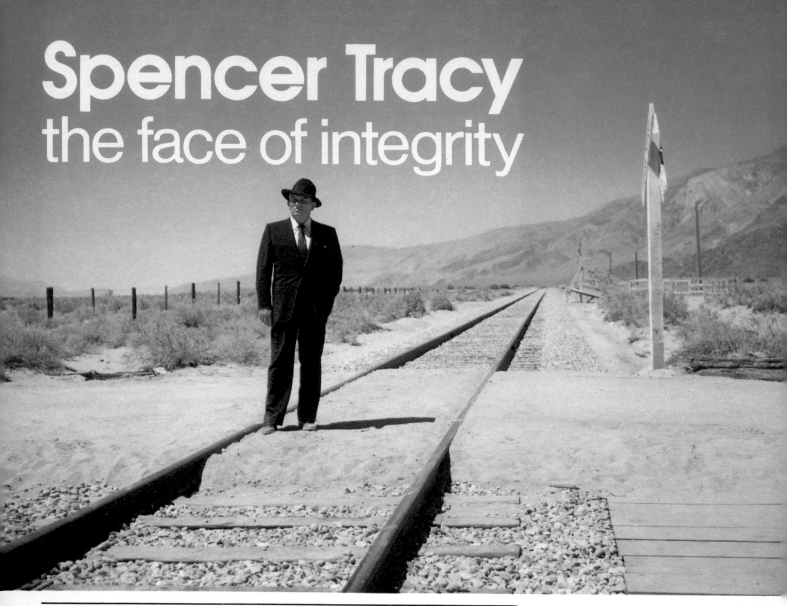

Chester Erskine, director of the Broadway play that projected Tracy to stardom, provides a penetrating insight into his old friend's work and character

'The best movie actor in the world', wrote an effusive journalist – just after Spencer Tracy had been nominated for an Academy Award for *Father of the Bride* in 1950. A lot of people, including most of his fellow actors, would agree to this. The notable exception was Spence himself.

'Now how can anybody declare me to be the best in the world? It's kind of silly. Like this Academy Award business, I'm damned pleased to be nominated and included amongst the other nominees, worthy actors all of them. That's enough of an honour for me. But if I should win, would that make me better than them? Of course not. A good performance depends on the role, and what the actor brings of himself to it. And him alone. I bring Spencer Tracy to it. Nobody else can bring Spencer Tracy to it because they're not me. I'm the best Spencer Tracy in the world. If they want to give me an award for that. I've truly earned it.'

This is a true insight into his own work – Spencer did not act roles, the roles acted Spencer. His performances were part of him. They *were* him.

He came upon this special approach during rehearsals of *The Last Mile* in 1930, a landmark play of the time in which society's right to take the life of even a murderer was questioned. It was directed by me in a new style of realism – one that I had successfully introduced into several previous productions, a true realism born out of a world in economic depression, a world impatient with euphemism. The play is about a convicted murderer awaiting execution in the death house of an American prison who chooses to die in violent protest rather than by passive compliance.

Spencer had previously appeared in a potpourri of plays in repertory and in New York. He was a promising actor who occasionally showed flashes of true talent. I had seen a few of his performances, and was not overly impressed by him as a candidate for the lead in *The Last Mile*. I was just about to dismiss him, when something about our too brief casting interview stayed with me. Since it was getting on to dinner-time I invited him to join me at a theatrical haunt. There, in a less strained atmosphere, I was suddenly made aware as we

were talking that beneath the surface, here was a man of passion, violence, sensitivity and desperation; no ordinary man, and just the man for the part.

On the play's opening night, I stationed myself at the back of the auditorium. I suddenly saw him, after a hesitant start, realize his power as he felt the audience drawn into the experience of the play and respond to the measure of his skill and the power of his personality. I knew that he had found himself as an actor, and I knew that he knew it. The play – and his performance – projected Tracy to permanent stardom.

It was inevitable, of course, that the new realism of the theatre would pass to films, then in the transitional period from silent pictures to dialogue pictures.

The film director John Ford came to New York and saw *The Last Mile*. He was fascinated by Tracy and invited him to make a picture. It turned out to be *Up the River* (1930), a slapstick prison comedy of no quality. It was an unfortunate start for Spencer. Fox, the company to which he was under contract, typecast him in similar roles and inferior material, though his performances rose far above the banal level of the films. Eventually a respite (inspired by film critics who complained of this misuse of his talent) came in the form of several interesting pictures. In particular there was *The Power and the Glory* (1933), a brilliant study by Preston

58

"I want you to kiss me — for luck!"

Opposite page: a mysterious, one-armed stranger (Tracy) arrives in a sleepy little town in Bad Day at Black Rock. *Above: Tracy as 'Bugs' Raymond, a truckdriver turned racketeer in* Quick Millions. *Right:* Woman of the Year, *Tracy and Hepburn's first film together. Below: Manuel (Tracy) sings Harvey (Freddie Bartholomew) a shanty in* Captains Courageous. *Below right: in* Mannequin *a failed businessman (Tracy) keeps the love of his wife (Joan Crawford). Bottom: Tracy as Father Flanagan in* Men of Boys' Town

Sturges of an industrialist's rise to power, in which Spencer came to maturity as a film actor in a role worthy of him.

This honeymoon period was short-lived, however, and Tracy found himself again assigned to pot-boiler fare. But he had endured enough by now and rebelled. Following his angry protests – and some bad behaviour – Fox released him from his contract. Shortly afterwards he signed for MGM. The second and crucial phase of his career had begun.

Louis B. Mayer, head of MGM, was not convinced that Spencer had sex appeal, so he was cast as a second lead to Clark Gable. Anyone acquainted with Spencer's private life could have reassured Mayer on this point, as Irving Thalberg, head of production, finally did. He freed Tracy from bondage to Gable and cast him opposite some of Hollywood's loveliest ladies, all of whom he was permitted to win by the script, and several of whom he won off-screen, regardless of script or permit.

MGM was soon aware that it had gained a genuine star worthy of 'first top billing over the title', as it is officially denoted. He did not stereotype himself into a single character or role to be repeated in various stories as other stars did. What is striking in a random selection of his film roles is their variety: the harried victim of Fritz Lang's *Fury* (1936); the loveable Portuguese fisherman of Kipling's *Captain's Courageous* (1937); the gentle Father Flanagan of *Boys' Town* (1938); the redoubtable Stanley in *Stanley and Livingstone* (1939); Pilon, a Mexican peasant not above a little petty larceny, in Steinbeck's *Tortilla Flat* (1942); Joe the pilot in *A Guy Named Joe* (1943).

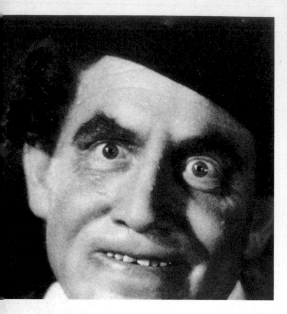

Above: Tracy dressed to kill as the evil Hyde in Dr Jekyll and Mr Hyde. *Above right: Tracy and Hepburn as rival – but married – lawyers in* Adam's Rib. *Right: a stormy family meal in* Guess Who's Coming to Dinner?

Tracy finished his contract at MGM with a masterful performance in *Bad Day at Black Rock* (1955) as the one-armed war veteran who uncovers a town's guilty secret; for this he received his fifth Oscar nomination. He next appeared in several distinguished films for Stanley Kramer with social themes close to Spencer's personal convictions. *Inherit the Wind* (1960) was a fictional account of the Dayton 'monkey' trial in Ohio during the Twenties, in which he played a lawyer, based on Clarence Darrow, who defends a teacher arraigned for teaching the Darwinian theory of evolution. In *Judgement at Nuremberg* (1961) he was the troubled judge at a Nazi war criminal trial. And *Guess Who's Coming to Dinner?* (1967), Tracy's last appearance, was a courageous story for the time, in which a couple, played by Tracy and Katharine Hepburn, come to accept the fact of a black husband for their daughter.

Spencer's famous partnership with Katharine Hepburn began in 1942 with *Woman of the Year*. It was an historic occasion, both professionally and personally. For the next 25 years they appeared together in a variety of films. Perhaps the best were two sophisticated comedies, *Adam's Rib* (1949) and *Pat and Mike* (1952).

When working, Spencer was very strict with himself. He examined the script carefully, defining his place in the story. He learned lines quickly, and asked for few if any changes. He relied on his ability to meet the requirements of the dialogue, no matter what. He did not go in for improvisation of any kind. He was a good listener in rehearsal and tried to do what was asked of him. Directors loved to work with him.

As a star, Tracy avoided publicity and interviews, which did not make him a favourite with the PR boys: 'I don't have to do those things,' he would say, 'Everybody knows me. They see me in pictures. That's who I am.'

But behind Spencer's strong, confident, craggy visage, there was an angry man disposed to self-destruction. When the strain became too intense he drank – drank fiercely to

oblivion. He was not the only actor so afflicted. There were others – too many others. We talked about this, and I suggested it might be because acting imposed on the actor the burden of being his own instrument so that he was in danger of becoming a split personality.

He smiled. 'Jekyll and Hyde? I played that part. Maybe. And maybe it's just that acting is no proper job for a grown man. I've never really felt comfortable about it.'

'But', he added, 'I wouldn't do anything else for the whole world!' CHESTER ERSKINE

Filmography
1930 Taxi Talks (short); The Tough Guy/The Hard Guy (short); Up the River. **'31** Quick Millions; Six Cylinder Love; Goldie. **'32** She Wanted a Millionaire; Sky Devils; Disorderly Conduct; Young America (GB: We Humans); Society Girl; Painted Woman; Me and My Gal (GB: Pier 13); 20,000 Years in Sing Sing. **'33** Face in the Sky; Shanghai Madness; The Power and the Glory (GB: Power and Glory); The Mad Game; A Man's Castle. **'34** Looking for Trouble; The Show-off; Bottoms Up; Now I'll Tell (GB: When New York Sleeps); Marie Galante. **'35** It's a Small World; Murder Man; Dante's Inferno; Whipsaw. **'36** Riffraff; Fury; San Francisco; Libeled Lady. **'37** They Gave Him a Gun; Captains Courageous; Big City. **'38** Mannequin; Test Pilot; Boys' Town. **'39** Stanley and Livingstone. **'40** I Take This Woman; Northwest Passage; Edison, the Man; Boom Town. **'41** Men of Boys' Town; Jekyll and Mr Hyde. **'42** Woman of the Year; Tortilla Flat; Keeper of the Flame; Ring of Steel (short; narr. only). **'43** A Guy Named Joe. **'44** The Seventh Cross; Thirty Seconds Over Tokyo. **'45** Without Love. **'46** untitled trailer for American Cancer Society (guest only). **'47** The Sea of Grass; Cass Timberlane. **'48** The State of the Union (GB: The World and His Wife). **'49** Edward, My Son (GB); Adam's Rib. **'50** Malaya (GB: East of the Rising Sun); Father of the Bride. **'51** Father's Little Dividend; The People Against O'Hara. **'52** Pat and Mike; Plymouth Adventure. **'53** The Actress. **'54** Broken Lance. **'55** Bad Day at Black Rock. **'56** The Mountain. **'57** Desk Set (GB: His Other Woman). **'58** The Old Man and the Sea; The Last Hurrah. **'60** Inherit the Wind. **'61** The Devil at 4 O'Clock; Judgement at Nuremburg. **'63** It's a Mad, Mad, Mad, Mad World; How the West Was Won (narr. only). **'67** Guess Who's Coming to Dinner?

'John Wayne, American'

John Wayne's long, final illness in the spring and summer of 1979 unleashed a tidal wave of American emotion. As the media constantly reminded everyone, Wayne was the man who carried 'true grit' over from the movie screen into real life: no self-respecting American could fail to be moved by the sight of the Duke, ravaged by 'Big C' but still a vast and imposing presence, looming up before the TV cameras at the 1979 Academy Awards ceremony. It *was* an awesome occasion:

'Oscar and I have something in common,' he said that night. 'Oscar first came to the Hollywood scene in 1928. So did I. We're both a little weatherbeaten, but we're still here and plan to be around for a whole lot longer.'

Two months later he was dead, but even as the old man slipped away Maureen O'Hara and Elizabeth Taylor fought desperately to win him a Congressional Medal of Honour, the highest tribute that can be paid to an American. It was the least President Carter could do, and the American people were able to take part in the medal-wearing too with the mass-minting of duplicate gold awards bearing the simple legend 'John Wayne, American'.

Above all others Wayne was the film star whom America had chosen as its symbol of strength, bravery, manliness, patriotism and righteousness in the post-war years. The film journalist Alexander Walker has persuasively argued in his book *Stardom* that Wayne 'was the most complete example of a star who has taken his politics into films and his films into public image'.

A Republican at Republic

The image of Wayne as the ultimate American fighting for right grew up during World War II when he played the war-hero in Republic's *Flying Tigers* (1942) and *The Fighting Seabees* (1944), and in the wake of Hiroshima when American military might was most in need of justification. In *Back to Bataan, They Were*

Marion Michael Morrison, a name to be conjured with – yet known by all. It is curious that women don't really take to him while men idolize him, and both will always see him sitting squarely on the back of a horse with a six-gun at his hip. However, given that as John Wayne he remained a superstar for over four decades, there **must have been more to him than that . . . or must there?**

Above: the Duke in jovial mood on set for The Cowboys *(1972).*

Expendable (both 1945), the fiercely jingoistic *The Sands of Iwo Jima* (1949), and John Ford's cavalry trilogy – *Fort Apache* (1948), *She Wore a Yellow Ribbon* (1949) and *Rio Grande* (1950) – he played war leaders who were tough, courageous, compassionate and *American*. Meanwhile, back at the Hollywood front Wayne, a staunch Republican and President of the Motion Picture Alliance for the Preservation of American Ideals, was taking an active part in running Communists out of the film capital – and colleagues out of their livelihood.

The films that also involved Wayne on the production side are those which most cohesively unite his movie and public images. *Big Jim McLain* (1952), which he co-produced, is pro-McCarthyist propaganda with Wayne as a tough HUAC investigator pursuing 'pinkos'; in *The Alamo* (1960), his first film as director, he played Davy Crockett defending Texas against Santa Anna's Mexican army – a martyr for American freedom; *The Green Berets* (1968) was his second stab at direction and is a vituperative pro-Vietnam War film in which he plays a mercenary routing the Vietcong. As 'pro-American' propaganda this is strong, sometimes unpalatable stuff, and he even recorded an LP called 'Why I Love America' with Robert Mitchum. Now there is a hint of bathos in that title, as there is in the whole of Wayne's over-inflated image as the last American hero, and it would be feasible to suggest that Wayne was aware of it. His Republicanism and anti-Communism (he had read widely

in Communist literature and in political science) were sincere, and he was a fervent supporter of Eisenhower, Goldwater and Nixon, but perhaps he knew too the power of talismans, bronze medals and movie images in the art of propaganda. Yet, strange as it may seem, in his greatest films Wayne's characters are not all that America would have them be.

South of the border . . .

If Wayne was and is a symbol of Americanism then, politically and socially, no other actor has done so much to undermine the self-righteous bluster of WASPish – White Anglo-Saxon Protestant – redneck values, both by espousing them and showing the neuroses nagging away at them. Wayne married three Spanish-Americans during his lifetime (so much for *The Alamo*) and eventually turned to Catholicism on his death-bed. If Ford, Hawks and the directors at Republic hadn't grabbed him for Westerns and war films in the late Forties and early Fifties, he might have been an effective star of *film noir*, so thoroughly ambiguous and troubled is his image when scrutinized. In fact Ford's *The Searchers* (1956) is a Western *film noir* with Wayne as a psychopath trapped in the alternatively light and dark landscape of his own mind. Even if Wayne *was* politically naive then surely he understood the dreadful frailty of his bloated, brow-beating characters and that the anger, insensitivity and spitefulness of Tom Dunson in *Red River* (1948), Sergeant Stryker in *The Sands of Iwo*

Above left: pioneers (Marguerite Churchill and Wayne) take to The Big Trail (1930) *in a realistic Western with 'grubby' actors. Above: Oliver Hardy and Wayne in* The Fighting Kentuckian (1949), *a tale of two men's fight to help French refugees settle in Alabama. Below: Sergeant Stryker (Wayne) leads an attack in* The Sands of Iwo Jima

Below: James Stewart, John Ford and Wayne pose for a publicity shot during the filming of The Man Who Shot Liberty Valance.

Jima and Tom Doniphon in *The Man Who Shot Liberty Valance* (1962) showed the bully and the tyrant in the hero who defends his flag at all costs. These characters are tired, unhappy men, soured and warped by their own experiences and plunged into crises of conscience which they can only solve by blasting their way out.

For all their self-sufficiency and arrogant confidence Wayne's movie characters – his American heroes – are lonely, sulky, ill-tempered and desperate. In good moods they tend to be bluff and patronizing – Wayne's grin is cracked, his eyes narrowed under his brow with suspicion. In bad moments they are monstrous; recall the incident in *Red River* when Dunson bounds across the trail, draws and shoots the cocky gunslinger without stopping his relentless march and lays into his young foster-son Matt (Montgomery Clift), a fury of flailing fists and mad temper. 'I never knew that big sonovabitch could act,' Ford said to Hawks after seeing *Red River*. As old men or neurotics Wayne was especially effective and knew exactly what he was about, as did Ford – his patron and mentor – and in *The Searchers*, *The Horse Soldiers* (1959), a wearied view of the Civil War, and *The Man Who Shot Liberty Valance*, they share the knowledge that the American Dream has become an American nightmare.

No Janet for John
On other levels Wayne's characters are equally ill at ease. It is significant that in many of his films he is essentially womanless. In *Red River* he leaves his girl behind (intending to return) but she is killed by Indians; *She Wore a Yellow Ribbon* finds him as a mawkishly sentimental widower who confides in his wife's grave; in *Rio Grande* he is estranged from his wife because he burnt down her home in the Civil War; in *The Searchers* the woman he loves is married to his brother; *The Man Who Shot Liberty Valance* sees him lose his girl to the man

who also usurps his heroism. The Wayne persona inevitably engenders sexual disharmony. For such an American hero Wayne frequently cut an impotent, asexual figure – so colossal that he swamps mere masculinity. He was certainly no Gable – after all, how many women find the Duke attractive? – and this is surely not the way the American male likes to view himself.

Of course there is an escape clause, for Wayne is seldom just a tyrant. After Dunson and Matt have fought themselves into the ground in *Red River*, Tess Millay (Joanne Dru) comes up to them: 'Whoever would have thought that you two could have killed each other?' she chides, and the loving father-son relationship is re-established. 'Come on Debbie, let's go home,' Ethan (Wayne) says to his niece instead of killing her as he had set out to do in *The Searchers*, and it was Jean-Luc Godard who pinpointed the secret of Wayne's appeal when he wrote, 'How can I hate John Wayne upholding Goldwater and yet love him tenderly when abruptly he takes Natalie Wood into his arms in the last reel of *The Searchers*?' Elizabeth Taylor was near the mark too when she said in that Congressional Medal plea, 'He is as tough as an old nut and soft as a yellow ribbon'.

Wayne was capable of an extraordinary

Above left: ace Indian hunter Lt. Col. Kirby Yorke, who involves himself in the Apache wars to protect the settlers in Rio Grande. *Above: Townsend Harris, a USA envoy sent to hostile Japan to arrange a trade treaty in* The Barbarian and the Geisha *(1958)*

Filmography
1927 The Drop Kick (uncredited) (GB: Glitter); Mother Machree (ass. prop man; +extra). **'28** Four Sons (ass. prop man); Hangman's House (uncredited). **'29** Words and Music; Salute; Men Without Women. **'30** Born Reckless (ass. prop man); Rough Romance; Cheer Up and Smile; The Big Trail. **'31** Girls Demand Excitement; Three Girls Lost; Men Are Like That (GB: The Virtuous Wife); The Deceiver; Range Feud; Maker of Men. **'32** The Voice of Hollywood No 13 (short) (announcer only); Shadow of the Eagle (serial); Texas Cyclone; Two-Fisted Law; Lady and Gent; The Hurricane Express (serial); The Hollywood Handicap (short) (guest); Ride Him Cowboy (GB: The Hawk); The Big Stampede; Haunted Gold. **'33** The Telegraph Trail; The Three Musketeers (serial; re-edited into feature Desert Command/ Trouble in the Legion, 1946); Central Airport; Somewhere in Sonora; His Private Secretary; The Life of Jimmy Dolan (GB: The Kid's Last Fight); Baby Face; The Man from Monterey;

Riders of Destiny; College Coach (GB: Football Coach); Sagebrush Trail. **'34** The Lucky Texan; West of the Divide; Blue Steel; The Man from Utah; Randy Rides Alone; The Star Packer; The Trail Beyond; The Lawless Frontier; 'Neath Arizona Skies. **'35** Texas Terror; Rainbow Valley; The Desert Trail; The Dawn Rider; Paradise Canyon; Westward Ho; The New Frontier; The Lawless Range. **'36** The Oregon Trail; The Lawless Nineties; King of the Pecos; The Lonely Trail; Winds of the Wasteland; The Sea Spoilers; Conflict. **'37** California Straight Ahead; I Cover the War; Idol of the Crowd; Adventure's End; Born to the West (reissued as Hell Town). **'38** Pals of the Saddle; Overland Stage Raiders; Santa Fe Stampede; Red River Range. **'39** Stagecoach; The Night Riders; Three Texas Steers (GB: Danger Rides the Range); Wyoming Outlaw; New Frontier; Allegheny Uprising (GB: The First Rebel). **'40** The Dark Command; Three Faces West; The Long Voyage Home; Seven Sinners (GB reissue title; Café of the Seven Sinners); Melody Ranch

Above: Wayne as a rancher enlisting the help of eleven small boys in The Cowboys *(1972). Above centre: a muddy reconciliation for* McLintock! *and estranged wife (Maureen O'Hara). Above right: Mattie (Kim Darby) and the marshal visit her father's grave in* True Grit

gentleness and chivalry and Ford was early to spot this when he cast him as Ringo, an outlaw who treats the whore Dallas (Claire Trevor) like a lady, in *Stagecoach* (1939). True, he was more accustomed to giving a girl a slap on the behind – most often Maureen O'Hara ('She's a big, lusty, wonderful gal . . . my kinda gal') who as the shrewish colleen of *The Quiet Man* (1952) warrants a playful smack and as the wife in *McLintock!* (1963) a thrashing with a shovel, but tenderness often undercuts his chauvinism. O'Hara seemed the only female capable of bringing out the erotic in Wayne – caught bare-legged with him in a graveyard during the thunderstorm in *The Quiet Man* she charges the air between them with sexual electricity – despite his having made three films with Dietrich. In *Three Godfathers* (1948) and *The Alamo* Wayne also showed a familiarity with babies and toddlers, but those scenes are best forgotten. Tenderness and warmth are an acceptable part of the noble savage's make-up; allowed to be maudlin Wayne was embarras-

sing to watch.

Ford's *Stagecoach* had caught the right mixture of gentleness and toughness, and even gives a glimpse of the uncertainty in the Wayne hero. The opening shot of Ringo twirling his rifle over his arm saluted his arrival as a star, but in fact Wayne was already a well-known face, albeit in B pictures.

Shooting to stardom

He was born Marion Michael Morrison in Winterset, Iowa, in 1907, the son of a druggist who took the family West to Glendale, Los Angeles, when Marion was nine. In 1925 he won a football scholarship to the University of Southern California where the Western star Tom Mix saw him. Mix offered him a job shifting props at Fox and there Wayne met John Ford who employed him as a herder of geese on the set of *Mother Machree* (1927). He appeared as an Irish peasant in Ford's *Hangman's House* (1928) and received his first screen credit as Duke Morrison for a bit-part in *Words and Music* (1929).

Then Raoul Walsh found him, changed his name to John Wayne and made him grow his hair long for the part of the wagon-train scout in the epic Western *The Big Trail* (1930). However, the film failed and despite a studio build-up, Wayne was consigned to B Westerns

at Columbia, Mascot, Monogram (for whom he made a series as Singin' Sandy beginning with *Riders of Destiny* in 1933) and eventually Republic on Poverty Row. But he kept in with Ford and was finally bullied by him into a starring career that lasted for forty years.

By the Sixties Wayne had become an American institution, too formidable a presence for the good of his films except when working with Ford or Hawks. The long-awaited Oscar came for his portrayal of Rooster Cogburn, the one-eyed war-horse in *True Grit* (1969), but it was a tribute to Wayne's long career rather than to that particular performance. With his last film, *The Shootist* (1976), man and myth became inseparable: the movie begins with a sequence of clips from old John Wayne movies, a requiem for the character he is playing – an ex-gunfighter dying of cancer – and for himself.

The giant's shadow remains

As movie stars go John Wayne is pretty well indestructible, being the survivor of some two hundred films. Even the uncovering of the darker side of his image seems to inflate him all the more, as did the cancer he subdued for so long. 'I hope you die,' Martin Pawley (Jeffrey Hunter) shouts in rage at Ethan in *The Searchers*. 'That'll be the day,' Ethan grins back. Like Ethan, Wayne endures and is here to stay whether he is wanted or not; a dubious American hero but undoubtedly a remarkable screen presence.

GRAHAM FULLER

(uncredited). '41 A Man Betrayed (GB: Citadel of Crime); Lady from Louisiana; The Shepherd of the Hills. '42 Lady for a Night; Reap the Wild Wind; The Spoilers; In Old California; Flying Tigers; Reunion in France (GB: Mademoiselle France); Pittsburgh. '43 A Lady Takes a Chance; In Old Oklahoma. '44 The Fighting Seabees; Tall in the Saddle. '45 Flame of the Barbary Coast; Back to Bataan; They Were Expendable; Dakota. '46 Without Reservations. '47 Angel and the Badman (+prod); Tycoon. '48 Red River; Fort Apache; Three Godfathers. '49 Wake of the Red Witch; The Fighting Kentuckian (+prod); She Wore a Yellow Ribbon; The Sands of Iwo Jima. '50 Rio Grande. '51 Operation Pacific; The Bullfighter and the Lady (prod. only); Flying Leathernecks; Jet Pilot. '52 The Quiet Man; Big Jim McLain (+co-exec. prod). '53 Trouble Along the Way; Island in the Sky (+co-exec. prod); Hondo (+co-exec. prod). '54 The High and the Mighty (+co-exec. prod). '55 The Sea Chase; Blood Alley (+exec. prod). '56 The Con-

queror; The Searchers. '57 The Wings of Eagles; Legend of the Lost (+co-exec. prod). '58 I Married a Woman (guest); The Barbarian and the Geisha. '59 Rio Bravo; The Horse Soldiers. '60 The Alamo (+dir; +prod); North to Alaska. '62 The Comancheros (+add. dir, uncredited); Hatari!; The Man Who Shot Liberty Valance; The Longest Day; How the West Was Won *ep* The Civil War. '63 Donovan's Reef; McLintock! (+exec. prod). '64 Circus World (GB: The Magnificent Showman). '65 The Greatest Story Ever Told; In Harm's Way; The Sons of Katie Elder. '66 Cast a Giant Shadow (+co-exec. prod). '67 El Dorado; The War Wagon (+co-exec. prod). '68 The Green Berets (+co-dir; +exec. prod); Hellfighters. '69 True Grit; The Undefeated. '70 Chisum; Rio Lobo. '71 Big Jake (+exec. prod). '72 The Cowboys; Cancel My Reservation (guest). '73 The Train Robbers (+exec. prod); Cahill – United States Marshal (+exec. prod) (GB: Cahill). '74 McQ. '75 Brannigan (GB); Rooster Cogburn. '76 The Shootist.